THE
FLOATING
WORLD

HOLOGRAMS BY RUDIE BERKHOUT

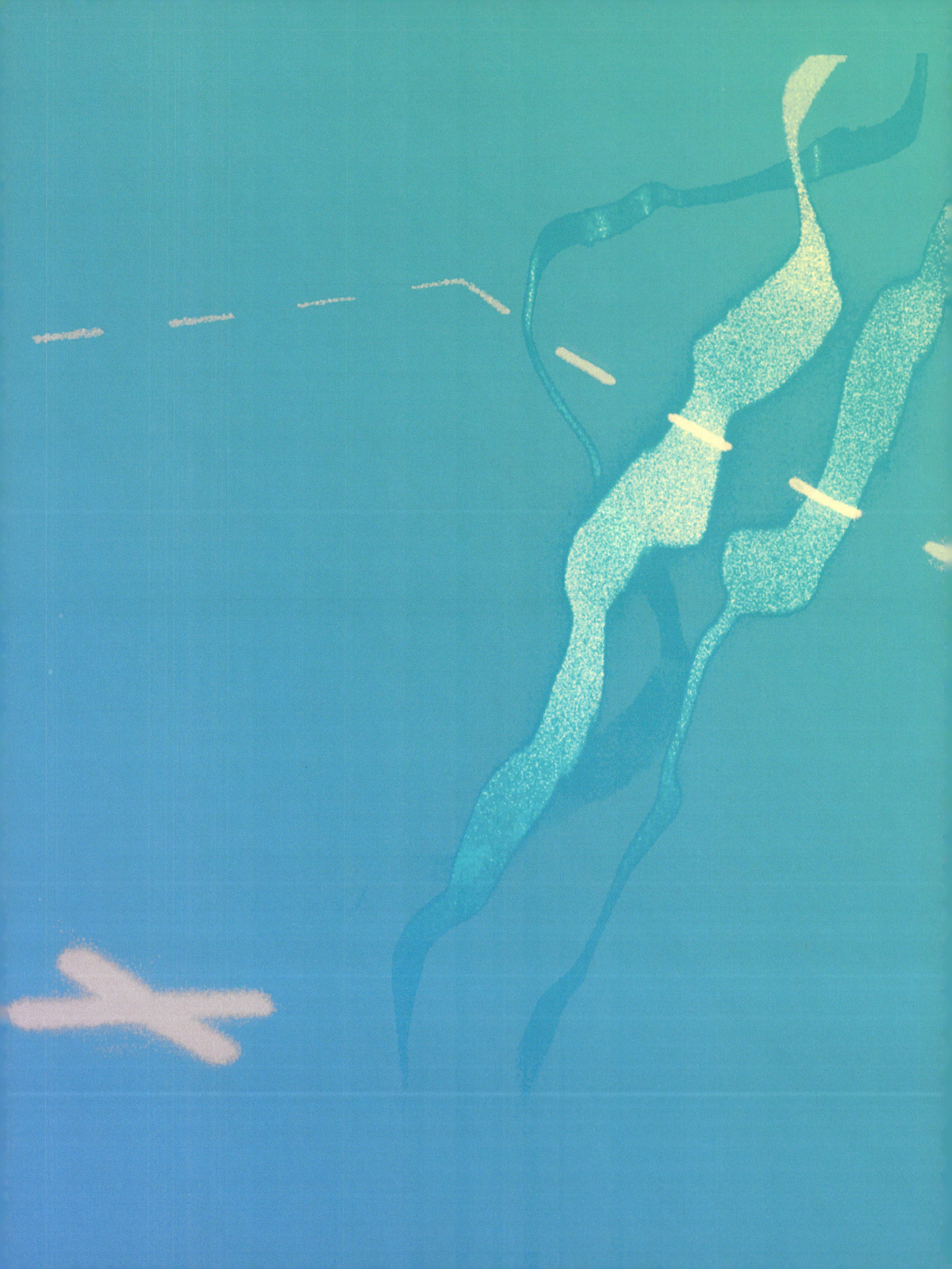

THE FLOATING WORLD

HOLOGRAMS BY RUDIE BERKHOUT

DANIEL BELASCO
EXHIBITION CURATOR

WITH CONTRIBUTIONS BY
RUDIE BERKHOUT
MARTINA MRONGOVIUS
SARA J. PASTI

SAMUEL DORSKY MUSEUM OF ART
STATE UNIVERSITY OF
NEW YORK AT NEW PALTZ

Published on the occasion of the exhibition *The Floating World: Holograms by Rudie Berkhout*, curated by Daniel Belasco, on display from February 6 – July 10, 2016 in the Sara Bedrick Gallery of the Samuel Dorsky Museum of Art, State University of New York at New Paltz.

The Dorsky Museum's exhibitions and programs are supported by the Friends of the Samuel Dorsky Museum of Art and the State University of New York at New Paltz. Additional support for *The Floating World* has been provided by The Rudie Berkhout Estate (www.rudieberkhoutcollection.com).

The Center for the Holographic Arts is supported by the Hologram Foundation with programming made possible by the New York State Council on the Arts with the support of Governor Andrew Cuomo and the New York State Legislature. (www.holocenter.org)

Published by the Samuel Dorsky Museum of Art
State University of New York at New Paltz
One Hawk Drive
New Paltz, New York 12561

Designed by Jeffrey Peltzman
Edited by Daniel Belasco, Curator of Exhibitions and Programs,
Samuel Dorsky Museum of Art, State University of New York at New Paltz
Printed by Lightning Source
Distributed by the State University of New York Press
(www.sunypress.edu)

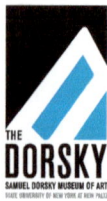
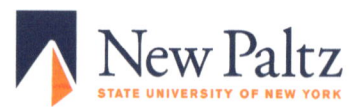
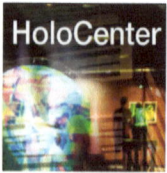

CONTENTS

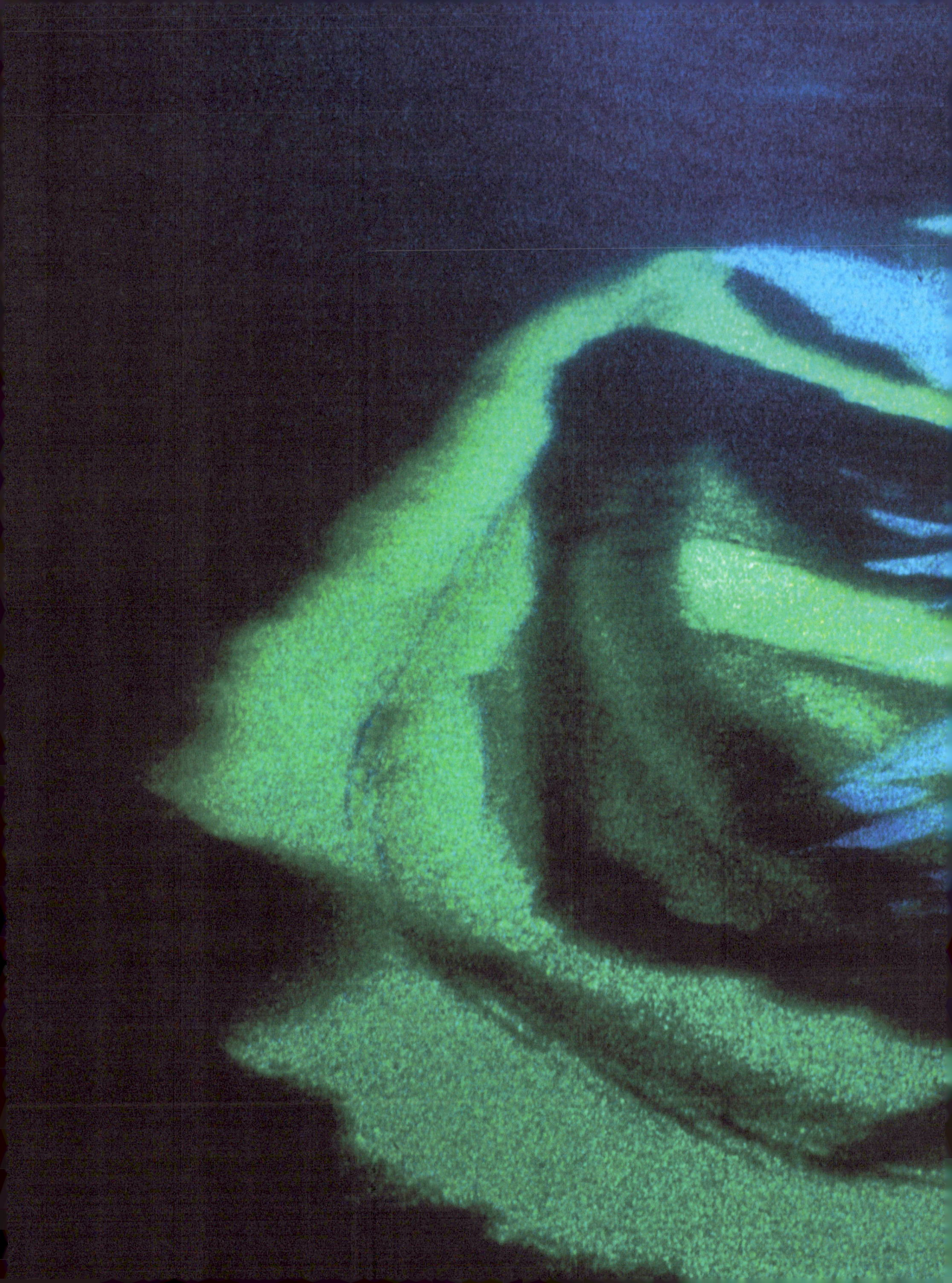

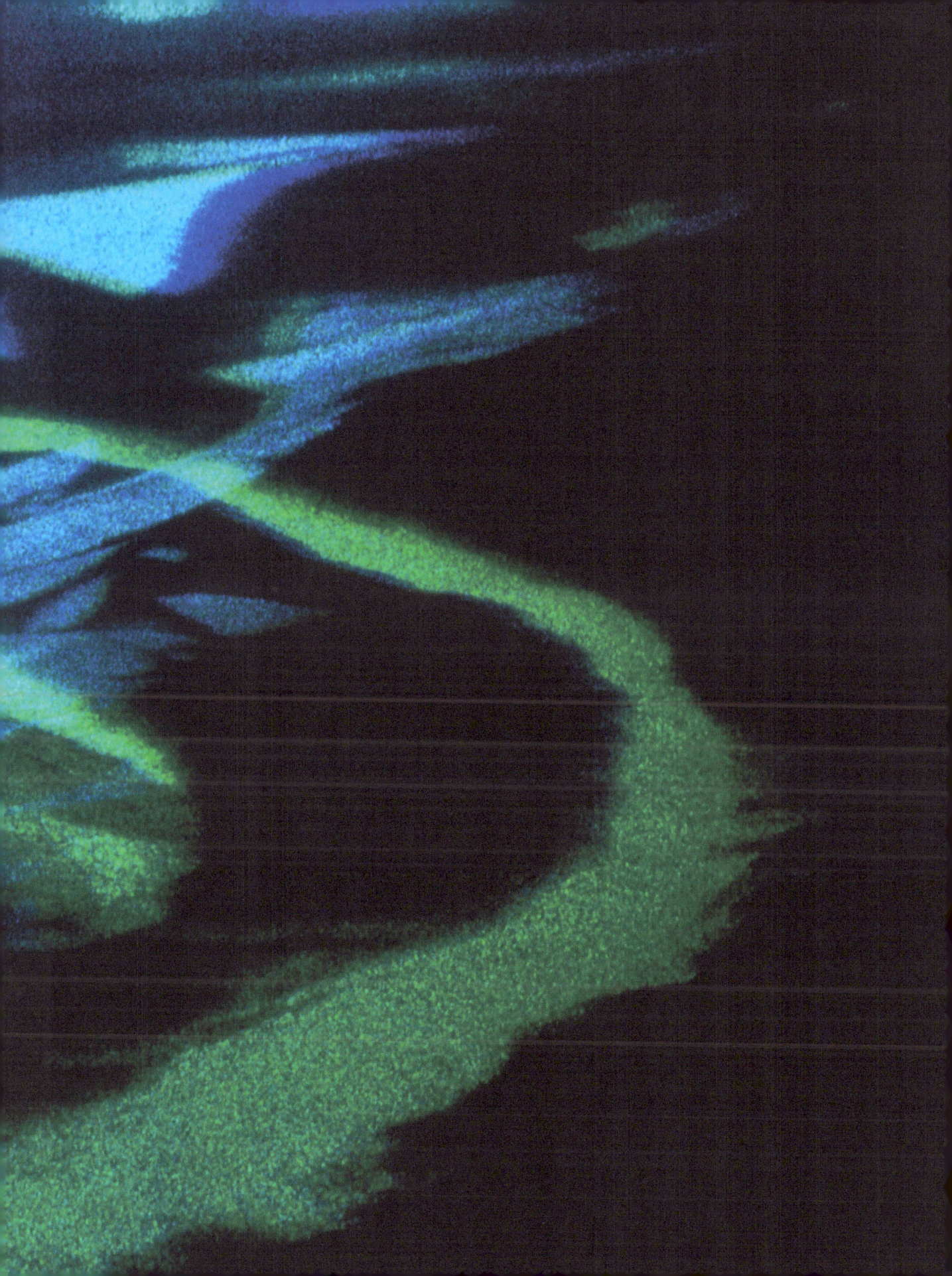

FOREWORD

SARA J. PASTI
THE NEIL C. TRAGER DIRECTOR
SAMUEL DORSKY MUSEUM OF ART

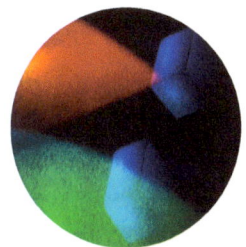

My first encounter with fine art holography took place in the mid-1980s when I visited the Museum of Holography in New York City. Like many others who visited the museum, I was intrigued by the technological mystery of the holograms, by their artistry rather than their art. The holographic portraits I saw there impressed me in the same way as did the waxworks of historical figures at Madame Tussauds Museum—they were amazingly accurate but a bit ghoulish in their representation of human likenesses. The Museum of Holography made such a lasting impact that until it closed in 1992 I made a point of bringing family and friends to the museum so they too could be witness to the magic of this unique medium.

These early experiences with holography were largely forgotten until I moved to the Hudson Valley and met Linda Law, a contemporary practitioner of holography and former curator of the Rudie Berkhout Collection. Linda provided me with an introduction to Rudie's work and also with an introduction to Hudson Talbott, who showed me more of Rudie's work. I was intrigued and inspired by Rudie's holograms, seeing in them a sophisticated understanding of art, a masterful command of the medium, and great beauty and visual presence. They were truly mesmerizing. When I learned that Rudie had lived in and been inspired by the Catskill Mountains—an area of focus for The Dorsky Museum—I knew that one day we would exhibit Rudie's holograms in the museum.

The Floating World is the first museum exhibition of Rudie's work in nearly two decades. It came into being through the generosity of Hudson Talbott, Rudie's long-time partner, and the efforts of Dorsky Museum curator Daniel Belasco, who turned out to be as intrigued by Rudie's work as I had been. I am grateful to Daniel for his scholarship, for the insight that he brings to the work, and for his organization of the exhibition and catalogue. I also thank Martina Mrongovius for her excellent essay, which offers an articulate presentation of the scientific basis of holography, and for her efforts in organizing the Rudie Berkhout archive.

Other individuals to whom I wish to extend my heartfelt thanks for their efforts on behalf of this project are Fred Berkhout, Michael Gabor, and Hart Perry, all of whom worked closely with the artist during this lifetime. Special thanks also go to Jeffrey Peltzman, the catalogue designer, who has made Rudie's art come alive on these pages. In addition, I would like to thank the following SUNY New Paltz colleagues for their assistance: Susan DeMaio Smutny, Visual Resources Librarian, Department of Art History; Catherine Herne, Assistant Professor, Department of Physics, Maggie Quinn and Amanda Henneberry, Dorsky Museum curatorial interns; Danielle Epstein, Dorsky Museum administrative intern; Arzu Yontar, Dorsky Museum graduate assistant; and Dorsky Museum staff members Janis Benincasa, Wayne Lempka, Jessica Lynn, Amy Pickering, and Bob Wagner.

Due to the continuing growth the commercial use of holograms as well as the development of the Holocenter on Governors Island, we may soon see a parallel growth of interest in fine art holography. Rudie Berkhout's strikingly beautiful holograms deserve to be recognized and studied as the starting point of any holographic art to come.

UNIFYING SCIENCE AND ART

RUDIE BERKHOUT

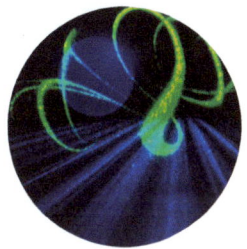

One of the beauties of this age is our discovery of the obsolescence of thinking in terms of opposites. Perhaps out of need for their specific developments, the arts, sciences, and philosophies have been previously perceived as separate cultural components. However, as the limitations in isolating the three units become increasingly apparent so does the boundless potential of their confluence. Holography, therefore, is the perfect medium to give this new union a chance to express itself.

For me, working in holography is not merely shifting back and forth between empirical knowledge and aesthetic judgments, but is also comprehending them as a part of a unified whole. I see myself as the medium through which the technology can express itself. I see technology as an integral part of nature and my function being to articulate its beauty. To do this requires an understanding of the behavior of light and its interaction with matter. Although studying the available texts about the properties of light has been helpful, most of my technical information has come from trial and error experimentation. Yet light's nature is subtle enough to easily elude mere facts and figures, and I find most often the best means of comprehending it is through my own intuition. Becoming one with light, following in thought its path through space and time gives me a framework of understanding from which the technical and aesthetic values seem to flow.

Beyond the requirements in approach to its creation, the visual impact of the hologram itself is perhaps a more succinct expression of this unification of art, science, and philosophy. As we adjust to what we are seeing, we are redefining and expanding our knowledge of visual possibilities. My hope is that the expansion of our perception's frontiers in one area may lead to questioning of all of its boundaries in general.

Reprinted from *New Spaces: The Holographer's Vision*. Philadelphia: The Franklin Institute Press, 1979.

WHERE IS THE IMAGE COMING FROM?

RUDIE BERKHOUT

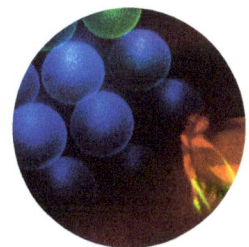

The holographic image originates at the glass surface of the hologram. The glass plate is covered with a very thin emulsion. In this emulsion are millions of tiny silversalt crystals acting like microscopic prisms. Each one of them bends the incoming light rays. All together they generate a complex wavefront of light that gives the viewer the spatial illusion, as if the light originates from an actual three-dimensional composition.

The hologram is an optical memory of a composition in space. It is recorded with laser light and made permanent with chemistry.

It is helpful to compare a hologram with a sound record. The sound record is an electronic memory of a composition in time. The "play-back" and "read-out" is accomplished by spinning the turntable, placing the needle on the record and listening to the work.

The "play-back" and "read-out" of the hologram is done by illuminating it with light and looking at the work from all the different angles (near and far, side to side and up and down). For me, working in holography is an exploration into many uncharted areas. New areas of visual perception and artistic possibilities.

Nature has given us this tool to learn from. However, we're also given the choice of how we wish to use this technology, so refined and awesome. We can again create "smarter" weapons to kill each other more effectively, or use it with the utmost respect and create more beauty and excitement to be shared by everyone. Obviously, I set out to explore holography with the latter in mind.

My hope is to reach the subtler levels of perception, holding up mirrors for thoughts, reflecting the magic we live in.

Reprinted from *The Holograms of Rudie Berkhout*, Milwaukee, WI: Patrick and Beatrice Haggerty Museum of Art, Marquette University, 1986.

THE FLOATING WORLD: HOLOGRAMS BY RUDIE BERKHOUT

DANIEL BELASCO
EXHIBITION CURATOR

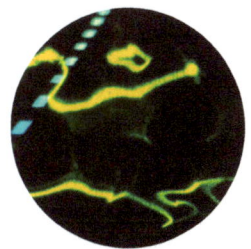

In 1984, nothing looked more like the future than a hologram. When *National Geographic* put a holographic bald eagle, embossed on foil, on the cover of 11 million copies of its March 1984 issue,[1] high technology had arrived in American mass culture, alongside the Macintosh and the compact disc [**Fig. 1**].[2] The worlds of finance and entertainment were ready for three-dimensional imaging; however, the tradition-bound art world never fully embraced the technology, despite the efforts of the first generation of practitioners to build institutions and develop a new critical language for holography.[3] The same year as the *National Geographic* cover, prominent art critic Grace Glueck called holography a "much-maligned medium."[4] Few serious holographic artists escaped this criticism and participated in the larger world of art and culture. Rudie Berkhout was one of them.

Born in Amsterdam in 1946, Berkhout moved to New York in 1974 and within a few years became a celebrated innovator in holography, which had only first become accessible to artists a decade earlier. Active on the downtown Manhattan scene, Berkhout socialized with performance artist Laurie Anderson and members of rock band The B-52s.[5] He enjoyed the esteem of his tight-knit world of holographers, and also found sympathetic contemporary art curators who included his holograms in group exhibitions alongside non-holographic works by artists as diverse as Larry Bell, Barbara Kruger, Judy Pfaff, and William Wegman.[6] The themes of these shows—beauty, technology, and audience participation—reveal the essential qualities of Berkhout's work, which have only grown in importance to contemporary art since the 1980s.

The Floating World focuses on a selection of the most significant transmission holograms—three-dimensional images that seemingly float from glass panels suspended in space or supported by a tripod—Berkhout made from 1978 to 1989. These years represented a peak period of his creativity as well as his professional recognition. Indeed, this period also marked a high point for general public interest in the futuristic potential of holography. "I see myself as the medium through which the technology can express itself," Berkhout wrote. That audacious position allowed him to break from the norms of the technology and use it as a plastic, sculptural medium.[7] His most accomplished works combine movement and shape, and expand vision so that a flat surface was not a limit, but a flexible interface that could reveal that the visual basis of reality lay in the mind and not the eye.

In 1948 Hungarian physicist Dennis Gabor, working in England, theorized a new way of capturing waves of light in what he called a hologram.[8] In the early 1960s, Emmett Leith and Juris Upatniek, working at the University of Michigan, applied the recently invented laser to realize Gabor's theory in the creation of the first wave transmission hologram. Unlike photography or naturalistic painting, which uses a one-to-one correlation of points of light in space to points on the photographic plane, holography records an image as the interference pattern between two beams of laser light converging at the same point on the picture plane. Special films with chemical treatments are able to capture these patterns. When the hologram is complete and the viewer sees it under optimal display and light conditions, the human eye perceives the interference between the two beams as volumes in space. In this regard, the hologram acts more like a lens than a photograph, redirecting lightwaves into what appears to be a three-dimensional form.[9] When Leith and Upatniek presented a hologram of a toy train engine—a quintessential image of childhood nostalgia—at the annual meeting of the Optics Society of America in 1964, they demonstrated how the new technology could powerfully stimulate imagination and memory [**Fig. 2**].[10]

The creative trajectory of holographic art is similar to that of computer art and animation. At first the technical and creative innovations were in the hands of the scientists who invented the medium. But soon artists found their way to the labs, collaborated with technicians, and eventually seized the technology for themselves. At this point, art and science parted ways, as each became subjected to their mutually exclusive criteria of form or function. Artists started working with holograms in the late

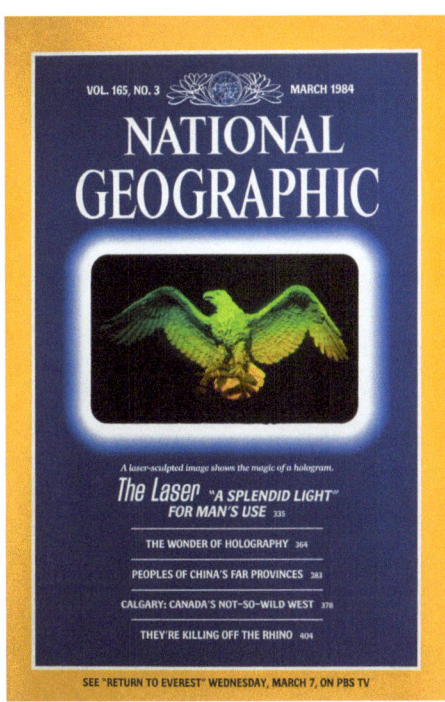

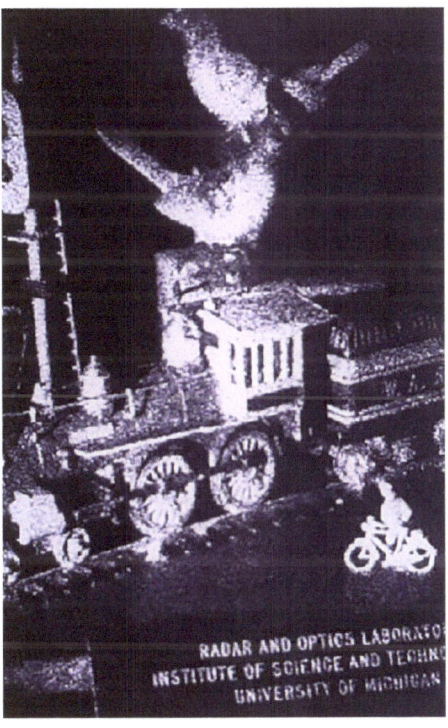

1960s. By the early 1970s in New York, Harriet Casdin-Silver, Ken Dunkley, Sam Moree, and Dan Schweitzer devoted themselves to holography, building their own personal or institutional labs, while artists like Bruce Nauman and Salvador Dalí hired technicians to translate their characteristic imagery into holograms. Similar pockets of innovation also emerged in Western European countries and American cities close to major universities, such as Boston and the San Francisco Bay Area.

Holographic technology and institutions were already in place when Berkhout was first exposed to the medium. Berkhout and his partner Hudson Talbott moved to New York City from Amsterdam, where they had worked as fashion and theatrical lighting designers in between extended travels in Asia.[11] A visit to the first major exhibition of artist holograms at the International Center for Photography in 1975 turned Berkhout on to holography.[12] The ability to work directly with a new technology thrilled him and offered a route to explore the intersection of science and art, which had fascinated him since his youth and early education in electrical engineering. Berkhout began taking classes in the New York School of Holography, making small reflection holograms on 4 x 5 inch plates, and became involved with the Museum of Holography after its founding by Rosemary (Posy) Jackson Smith in 1976.[13] Berkhout threw himself into learning everything he could about the rapidly evolving field. He also became a partner in the New York Holographic Film

Fig. 1 *National Geographic*, March 1984. Reflection hologram on offset print, bounded paper. Courtesy National Geographic.
Fig. 2 Juris Upatnieks and Emmett N. Leith. *Train and Bird*, 1963. Laser transmission hologram; glass, 5 x 4 in. MIT Museum, MOH-1976.01.

Company, founded by filmmaker Hart Perry, serving as Vice President. There he helped invent a holographic film printer and a time-lapse method, resulting in filmstrip-like reflection holograms such as the blooming lily, *Ruben* (1977) [**Fig. 3**].[14] Ever seeking new materials and techniques, Berkhout also maintained correspondence with many scientists working around the world, such as Stephen Benton and N.J. Phillips in England, to compare notes about the chemistry of processing, and had a residency in the Brown University physics department, sponsored by Hendrik Gerritsen.[15]

Berkhout soon moved away from the gee-whiz illusionism of representational imagery that dominated holography then, as it does now. His aesthetic breakthrough came with the *Photon Studies* of 1978 [**Plate 1**], in which Berkhout tackled what he called the problem of spectral light. Laser-made holograms use spectral light, pure unmixed (rainbow) colors, which can appear garish and unnatural. In an article in *Leonardo* magazine, Berkhout compared his spectral light holograms to synthesizer music, also a new electronic medium at the time. One note could sound cold, but several together form a rich chord. Similarly, Berkhout layered light so that several colors could be viewed simultaneously. Focusing on multi-color image "harmonics," Berkhout sought objects and images that translated well in monochromatic spectral color.[16] His *Photon Studies* consist of holograms made by "drawing" with the points of light.[17] Suggesting the micro- and macro-cosmos, they remind us that holography was invented by a scientist researching new imaging systems for an electron microscope.

After exploring point and line in the *Photon Studies*, Berkhout played with geometrical shape in *12mW Boogie* [**Plate 2**].[18] Repeated patterns of circles, squares, and triangles oscillate across the surfaces of three holograms, on three glass panels mounted in a handmade wood frame. The colors shift from green to blue to red as the viewer moves his or her head and body left and right, forward and back, up and down. The title references both the work of Dutch artist Piet Mondrian, who also found a home in New York City, and the disco craze of Berkhout's time. The viewer has to boogie to fully experience the work.

Determined to make a living as an independent artist, Berkhout produced holograms in editions of nine, a fortunate number for him. In late 1978 he sold copies of *12mW Boogie* and several *Photon Studies* to collectors in England, Germany, and the Museum of Holography. The proceeds of $2,000 were enough to rent a 600 square foot basement at 91 Fifth Avenue and build his first laboratory.[19] A homespun,

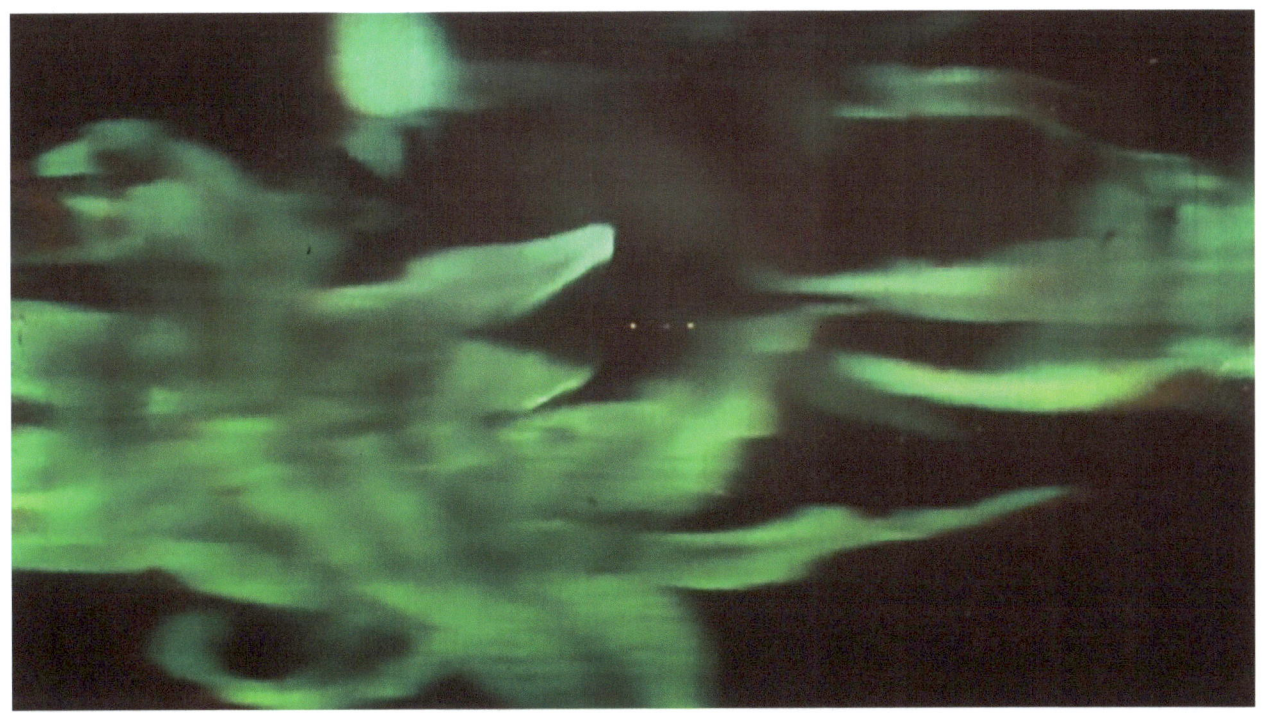

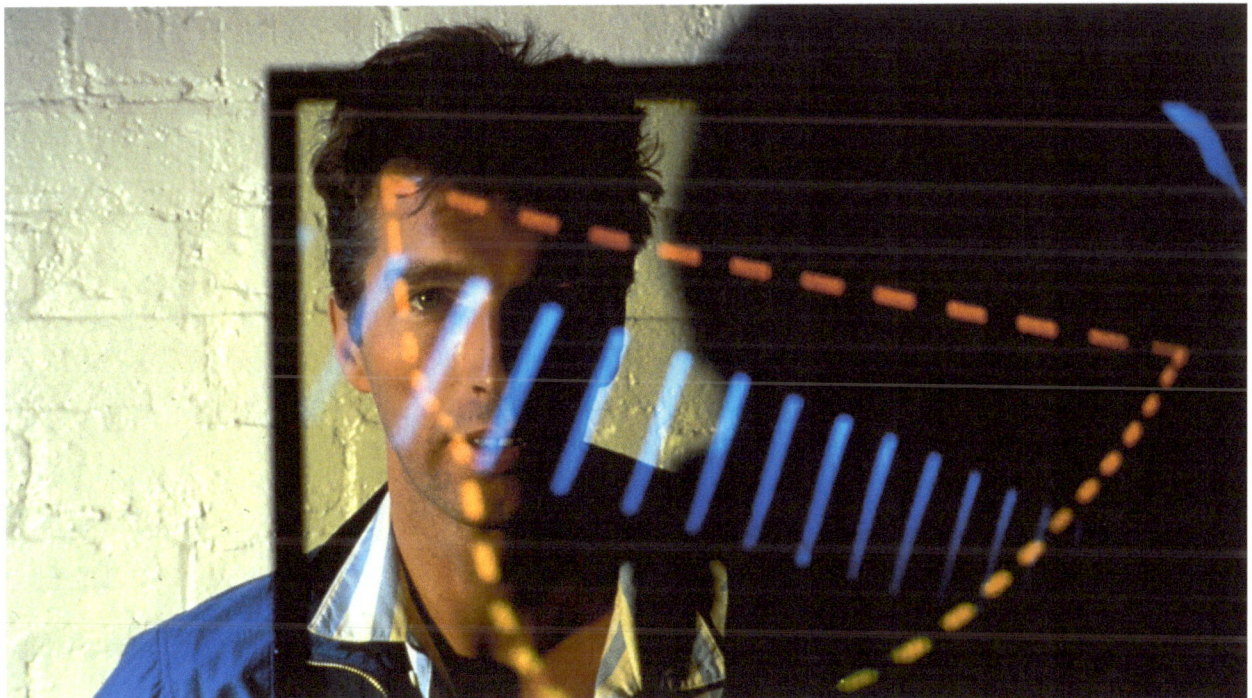

Fig. 3 Rudie Berkhout. *Ruben*, 1977. 120° integral stereogram (Multiplex); film, 6 x 9 in. MIT Museum, MOH-1977.37.02
Fig. 4 Rudie Berkhout and *Delta II*, 1982. Courtesy Rudie Berkhout Estate.

jury-rigged artist holography studio is like no other. Whereas painters avoid darkness, video artists avoid sound, and photographic developers avoid daylight, holographers avoid vibration. They pour concrete floors and construct multi-ton concrete work tables on movement-dampening materials. The table has to float above the floor not to be rattled by city movement.[20] This allows for the great precision required to reunite a split laser beam in a single point to make the hologram.

Settled into his new studio, Berkhout began a remarkable run of creativity. Works like *Future Memories* (1979) [**Plate 3**], *Transfer 137* (1980) [**Plate 4**], and *Event Horizon* (1980) [**Plate 5**] bring us into an alternate universe. Animated runes, deeply recessed dotted lines, and rippling waves evoke a cosmic space of myth, travel, and spiritual longing. They provide viewers with a tangible experience of the stark beauty of the environment of the future, distilling a spatial vision later writ large in movies such as *Blade Runner* (1982) and *Tron* (1982). Working with modest equipment and resources, Berkhout accepted the dimensional limitations of the holographic film that he was using, first 8 x 10 inches and then 12 x 16 inches when that size became available around 1981. He discovered that he could achieve greater depth and movement if his holograms focused on a few richly evocative images.

Berkhout's following series eschewed landscape entirely. He isolated a small number of forms and objects and arranged them in poetic compositions. There is a condensation and clarification of vocabulary in what can be called the Asia series from 1981, which includes *Ukiyo* [**Plate 6**], *Kyoto*, *Kuan Yin*, and *Toba* [**Plate 7**]. They combine memories of Berkhout's extensive travels in Indonesia, Japan, and Hong Kong, while also evoking the technological fundamentals of the medium of holography. *Delta II* (1982) [**Fig. 4**] and *Delta IV* (1982) [**Plate 8**] build on these works, while also adopting the dotted line used in plotting lasers as a self-referential element acknowledging the making of the holograms, a classic postmodern touch.

Berkhout aspired for the viewer to have a participatory experience of his work, always trying new ways to expand and enhance the viewer's interaction with his art. To fully engage with Berkhout's transmission holograms, we must move our bodies, performing a strange choreography to set them in motion before our eyes. Berkhout wrote "the viewer is like the needle of a record player, playing the hologram."[21] The music reference is not idle, as Berkhout preferred to present his holograms with a soundtrack of compositions by Brian Eno, Philip Glass, and others, which he

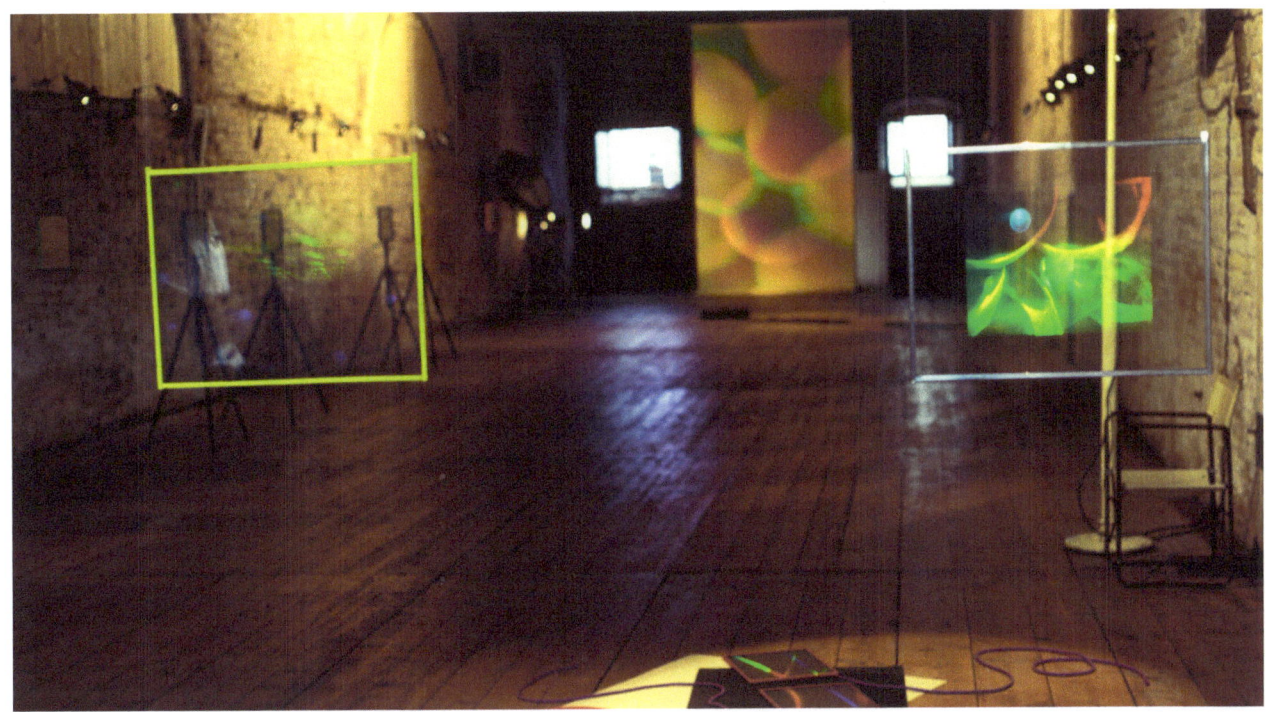

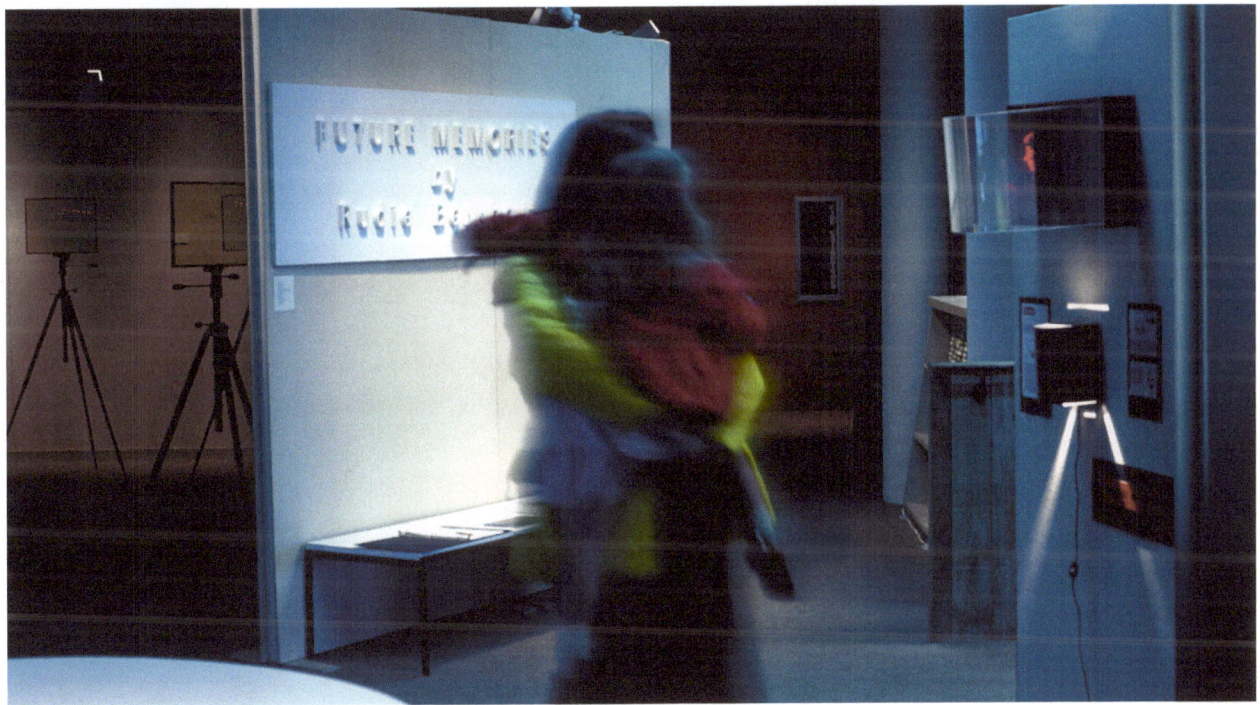

Fig. 5 Installation view of *Rudie Berkhout*, Fortuny Palace, Venice, 1982. Courtesy Rudie Berkhout Estate.
Fig. 6 Installation view of *Future Memories* exhibition, Port Washington Library, New York, 1984. Courtesy Rudie Berkhout Estate.

appropriated for his own purposes and mixed on audiotapes.[22] Berkhout hoped that the electronic and minimalist music allied with his abstract imagery would promote an experience of synesthesia to transport the viewer from the naturalistic realm to multisensory awareness of art and science. "Holography is a high-tech crack in the wall for adults [to dream]," Berkhout said in *The New York Times*.[23]

Critics and curators wisely understood that the interactive, sculptural aspects of Berkhout's transmissions made them ripe for multimedia exhibition. In 1981, Berkhout presented three transmission holograms in *The Art of Reaction* at the Katonah Art Gallery, a three-person exhibition (with new media artist Anthony Martin and sound artist Liz Phillips) showcasing artists who used technology for audience participation. Observed critic Vivien Raynor: "the spectrum colors depend on the height of whoever is looking at them."[24] However, some critics recognized the holography could only exist as an intimate art experience. David Hlyinsky wrote in 1979, "transmission holograms mimic sculpture in their display requirements but are hard-pressed to compete with the 'monumental' presence of traditional sculpture."[25] Mindful of this challenge, Berkhout made large-scale installations when given the chance. At the Fortuny Palace in Venice, timed with the Biennale of 1982, he mounted an installation that resembled a holographic De Stijl interior [**Fig. 5**]. Reflection holograms were placed on the floor, set at 45-degree angles on black and white color panels, and transmission holograms were suspended from the ceiling and mounted on tripods. The holograms' geometric forms and use of primary colors have an elementary quality, arranged in the stylish asymmetry of New Wave design.

By 1983, Berkhout returned to representation, starting with his own image. A self-portrait in profile became an element of several works, including *Wavering* (1983) [**Plate 9**], which is displayed on a tripod at a 45-degree angle. *Wavering* marked a shift from the geometric back to the organic in which Berkhout became more romantic and confident with his use of personal symbolism. Around this time Berkhout was fully recognized as a leader in holographic art. He organized a solo exhibition, *Future Memories*, which traveled to five museums and libraries, attracting local media and public attention at every stop [**Fig. 6**].[26] His holograms were published on the covers of several books and catalogues on the subject [**Fig. 7**].[27]

Throughout this period there were ups and downs. Berkhout lost the lease to his Manhattan studio at the end of 1983. After several months, however, he established a new, larger, studio with good light and a sand table, in the basement at 223 West 21st Street in Chelsea. Longing for nature, he also began to enjoy extended stays in the Catskill Mountains. Berkhout commemorated the inspirational landscape in a major two-panel hologram, *The New Territories* (1984) [**Plate 10**]. The mountainous shapes were created by lasers reflecting off sculpted sand, and depict a panoramic view far different than the deep focus runway suggested in *Transfer 137*. With *The New Territories*, Berkhout announced his departure from the artificiality of urban imagery and joined the company of Thomas Cole and the Hudson River School, seeking spiritual and aesthetic renewal in the American landscape. In 1985 Berkhout and Talbott purchased a farmhouse in Cairo, NY, which solidified their links to the Hudson Valley environment and cultural scene.[28]

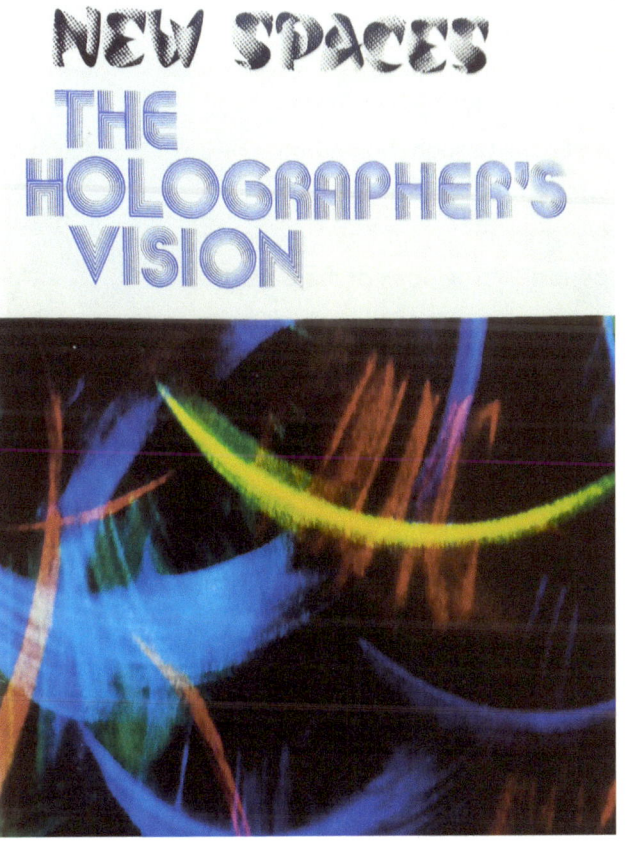

At this time, Berkhout also participated in the ferment of contemporary art. In the group show *Dutch Artists in New York*, Berkhout's *Deltawerk* (1982) hung gracefully with textiles and paintings [**Fig. 8**]. Curt Marcus, director of the Borgenicht Gallery, included Berkhout in a seven-artist group show in 1984. Berkhout's five transmission pieces hung alongside the media-based photomontages of Barbara Kruger, the nature drawings of Michael Zwack, and the acerbic collages of Sue Coe. This stimulating context opened up new possibilities for considering the latent content of Berkhout's work as a critique of modernism by applying its formalist precepts to a scientific technology. Critic Edward Lucie-Smith wrote that Berkhout was among the

Fig. 7 *Sketching Away* on the cover of *New Spaces: The Holographer's Vision*, The Franklin Institute Press, 1979.

few artists who were presenting "the spectator with an experience of seeing which is possible only in this medium."[29] By maximizing the capability of a hologram to be a hologram, and not a substitute for reality, he earned his renown.

David Katzive, former director of the adventurous Artpark in Western New York, served as director of the Museum of Holography from 1984–1986, expanding its exhibition program by including diverse artists working beyond the medium.[30] Museum curator René Paul Barrilleaux sought to create an integrated museum program in what was then known as intermedia art. Both museum staff and community members did not consider these projects to be fully successful, yet in retrospect they stand as notable attempts to expand the definition of art, using holography as a lever to pry apart an emotional space between aesthetics and technology.[31]

Spending more and more time in the Catskills inspired Berkhout to intensify his study of natural forms and materials after shunning them in the late 70s and early 80s. *Break Even* (1989) continued his experiments with sand as a reflective, textured surface for bolts of light or skeins of color. Berkhout also used personal objects as sources of holographic imagery, such as a piece of coral brought home from a visit to Posy Jackson in *Exuma* (1988)[32] and a torn paper self-portrait, in *Union* (1988). Berkhout later described this last phase of the transmissions, from *The New Territories* to *Breakthrough* (1990) [**Fig. 9**], as his "middle period." [33] The apex of the public recognition of Berkhout's transmission holograms may have been the exhibition *New Directions in Holography* at the Whitney Museum of American Art in 1991. Curated by Barilleaux, it included six transmission holograms by Berkhout and one five-part installation by Michael Wenyon and Susan Gamble. This turned out to be Berkhout's last major presentation of holograms in New York City in his lifetime.

The Whitney show, which should have been a triumph, gained a sigh. In *The New York Times* critic Paul Hagen called holography a "fabulous freak" with great strengths and great limitations.[34] The closing of the Museum of Holography in 1992, and the transfer of its collection and archive to the MIT Museum, represented the end of an era. In the early 1990s, upon completion of his dream lab in the basement of a house he built across the street from the farmhouse, Berkhout moved permanently to the Catskills and dedicated his efforts to extending the dimensional space of abstract reflection holograms of light waves. During this last phase of his career, Berkhout used reflection holograms as building blocks in cascading three-dimensional installations.

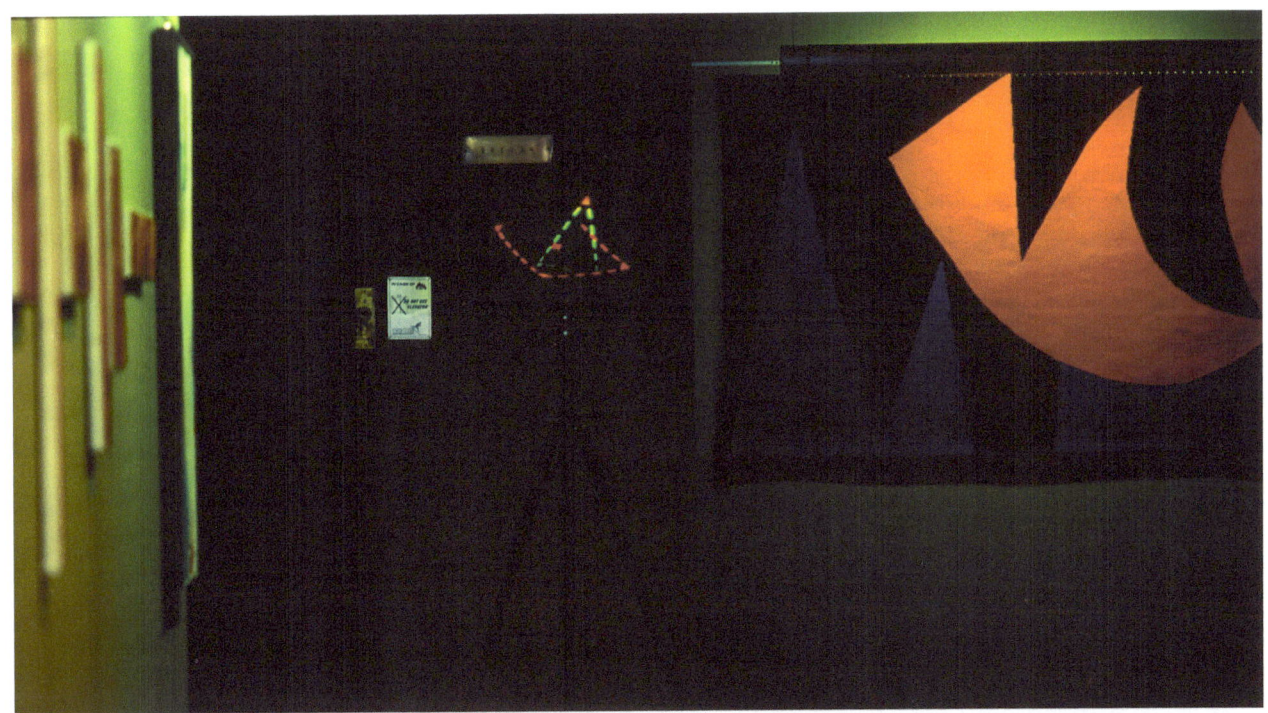

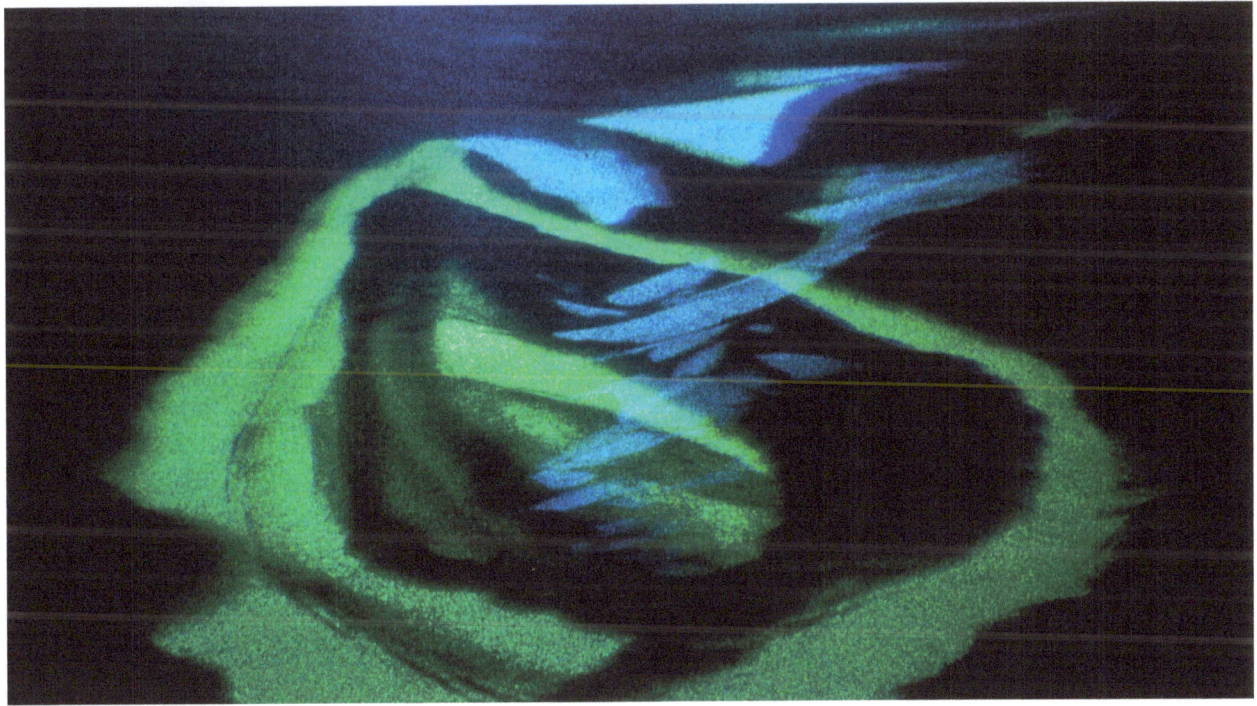

Fig. 8 Installation view of *Deltawerk* in *Dutch Artists in New York*, Kling Gallery, Philadelphia, 1982. Courtesy Rudie Berkhout Estate.
Fig. 9 Rudie Berkhout. *Breakthrough*, 1990. Transmission hologram: silver-halide glass plate. 12 x 16 in. Courtesy Rudie Berkhout Estate.

Berkhout created *Light Rain*, a commissioned installation of eight 30 x 30 inch reflection holograms, in a new atrium at the University of Wisconsin–Madison College of Engineering in 1992 [**Fig. 10**].[35] He completed a similar commission of 12 reflection holograms, installed with paintings by Ward Bos, entitled *Odyssey 2001*, for Bank of America in Charlotte, North Carolina, in 2001 [**Fig. 11**]. Berkhout continued to experiment with environmental installations up to his death from a heart attack in 2008.

Art holography has remained a vital, if small, area of creativity. The Center for Holography in New York City is one of the rare public venues for making and showing artistic holograms. But the hologram is at risk of being considered an artifact of the past, as suggested by the title of a recent art museum exhibition of the medium: *Pictures from the Moon*.[36] Ubiquitous digital technologies have increasingly usurped the analog world and revived public interest in full-scale three-dimensional imaging, especially in theatrical entertainment, but also in medicine, science, and archaeology. In the second decade of the 2000s, pop concert goers began to experience life-sized pseudo "holograms" (really two-dimensional images projected on three-dimensional surfaces) of deceased performers alongside flesh and blood singers, such as the famed "appearance" of Tupac Shakur at the Coachella Festival in 2012. Berkhout had foreseen this change in the culture, and in the 1990s shifted his practice to environmental design with holograms and custom lighting, founding the company Novia Lighting Design. Berkhout's transmission holograms are an important part of the story of techno-utopianism and the open source movement in art, linking the cybernetics of the 1960s to the hacker and maker cultures of today.

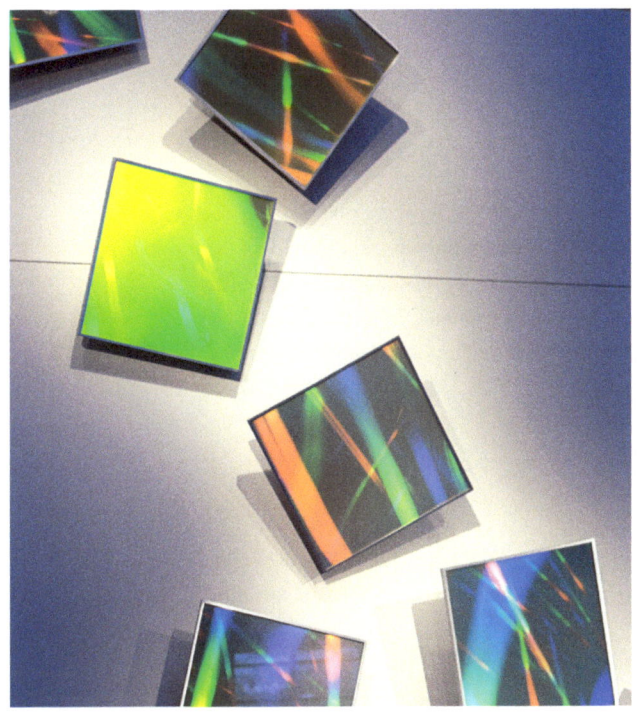

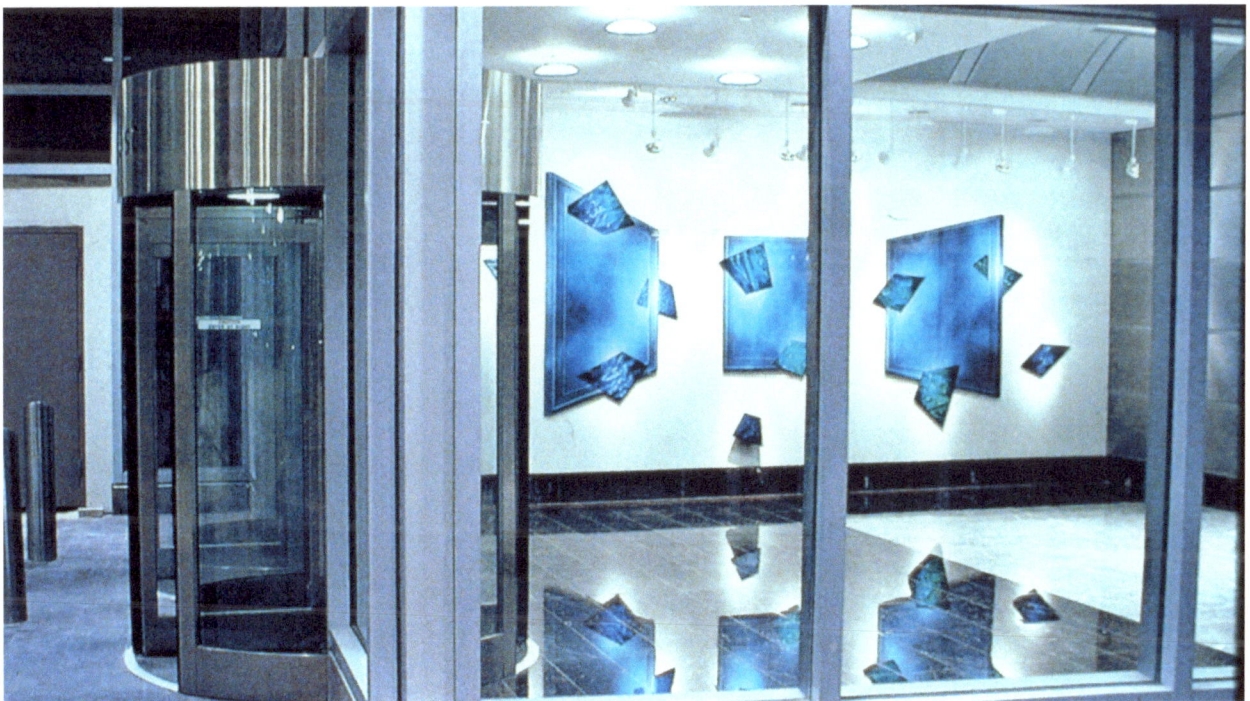

Fig. 10 Rudie Berkhout. *Light Rain*, Madison, WI, 1992. Courtesy Rudie Berkhout Estate.
Fig. 11 Rudie Berkhout and Ward Bos. *Odyssey 2001*, Charlotte, NC, 2001. Courtesy Rudie Berkhout Estate

Notes

1. In letter to David M. Seager, Art Director of National Geographic Book Service, Berkhout proposed to make a hologram, inspired by Leonardo's *Vitruvian Man*, with Stephen Benton and Polaroid for the cover of *National Geographic*. Rudie Berkhout to David M. Seager, January 9, 1984. Rudie Berkhout Archive, Cairo, NY. The actual published hologram was produced by Eidetic Images, founded by Ken Haines.

2. The issue included a photograph and caption of Berkhout's exhibition *Future Memories*. See H. John Caulfield, "The Wonder of Holography," *National Geographic* 165, no. 3 (March 1984): 364–365.

3. A hologram of an element of a Lucas Samaras relief appeared on the cover of *Artforum* (Summer 1985). It was made by Dan Schweitzer.

4. Grace Glueck, "Art," *The New York Times*, June 1, 1984.

5. Berkhout's *Planet Claire* (1979) is titled after the B-52s song.

6. Such as *Beyond Object* curated by Philip Yenawine at the Aspen Art Center (1980), *The Art of Reaction* at the Katonah Art Gallery (1981), and *Eddies* curated by David Katzive at the Visual Arts Museum, School of Visual Arts (1985).

7. Berkhout, "Unifying Science and Art," in *New Spaces: The Holographer's Vision*, Philadelphia: The Franklin Institute Press, 1979.

8. Margaret Benyon, "On the Second Decade of Holography as Art and My Recent Holograms," *Leonardo* 15, no. 2 (Spring 1982): 89–95.

9. Thanks to Hart Perry for clarifying the definition of a hologram and its creation.

10. The *Train and Bird* hologram is in the collection of MIT Museum, accessioned as part of the Museum of Holography collection.

11. Rudie Berkhout, "Holography: Exploring a New Art Realm—Shaping Empty Space with Light," *Leonardo* v. 22 n. 3 / 4 (1989): 313.

12. *Holography '75: The First Decade* was co-curated by Rosemary Jackson and Jody Burns.

13. Also that year, the Museum of Holography presented 20 holograms, including one by Berkhout, at the Museum of Modern Art's *Picture This*, a one-night educational program for high school and college students.

14. According to Hart Perry, email June 2015.

15. Correspondence with Gerritson, Benton, Phillips, and others in the Berkhout Archive.

16. Berkhout, *Leonardo*, 314.

17. A related work is *Sketching Away* (1979).

18. A related work is *To the Boogie Fun* (1978).

19. Al Razutis, "Conversation with Rudie Berkhout," 1985. The address inspired the title of Berkhout's well-known hologram *91F* (1979).

20. One artist in New York City would work in the late night, and time his holograms with the traffic lights down the end of the block. With a friend serving as look out, as soon as the light turned red, the holographer would get the okay to turn on his laser and direct it toward to object to be rendered three dimensionally.

21. Berkhout, quoted in *Light Dimensions: The Exhibition of the Evolution of Holography* (London: Ardentbrook, 1977), 70.

22. Berkhout's playlist for his exhibitions in the mid-1980s was: Brain Eno, David Behrman, David Casper, Deuter, The Harmonics Choir, Henry Wolff and Nancy Hennings, Jon Bernoff and Marcus Allen, K. Leimer, Laraaji, Matthew Young, Paul Horn, Peter Michael Hamel, Philip Glass, Steve Reich, Steve Halpern, Tony Scott, and Walter Carlos. None of Berkhout's original mixtapes are presently located.

23. Quoted in "New Wave of Holographers Work to Expand the Art," *The New York Times*, July 22, 1984.

24. Vivien Raynor, "Art; Technology as a Medium for Artists," *The New York Times*, February 22, 1981.

25. Quoted in Benyon, "On the Second Decade."

26. Between 1983 and 1985 *Future Memories* appeared in the Science Museum of Virginia, Norfolk, VA; James Prendergast Library, Jamestown, NY; Port Washington Library, Port Washington, NY; Lakeview Museum of Arts and Sciences, Peoria, IL; and the Davenport Art Gallery, Davenport, IA.

27. *Sketching Away* was on the cover of *New Spaces: The Holographer's Vision* (1979). *Event Horizon* appeared on Don McNair's *How to Make Holograms* (Blue Ridge Summit, PA: Tab Books, 1983), but Berkhout was unhappy with the reproduction quality.

28. Thanks to Hudson Talbott for clarifying this chronology.

29. Edward Lucie-Smith, *Art of the Seventies* (Ithaca, NY: Cornell University Press, 1980), 116.

30. Katzive's show at the School of Visual Arts included Berkhout along with Judy Pfaff, Charles Ross, and Salli Zimmerman.

31. See René Paul Barrileaux, "Holography and the Art World," *Leonardo* 25 no. 5 (1992): 417–418. See also Linda Law, "Museum of Holography: Conflict and Change," *Wavefront* (Fall 1986).

32. Per Hudson Talbott.

33. He wrote that *Awakening* (1985) is one of his favorites from this period. Rudie Berkhout, email to Jonathan Ross, April 19, 2002. Berkhout Archive.

34. Charles Hagen, "The Case for Holograms: The Defense Resumes," *The New York Times*, November 29, 1991.

35. Ina Pasch, "Energetic Art: Artist Seeks Impact through Dazzling Light Sculpture," *Wisconsin State Journal*, October 11, 1992. Berkhout Archive.

36. *Pictures from the Moon: Artists' Holograms 1969–2008*, at the New Museum, New York, 2012. Only reflection holograms were in the show.

THE CRAFT OF RUDIE BERKHOUT'S HOLOGRAPHY

MARTINA MRONGOVIUS, PHD
DIRECTOR, CENTER FOR THE
HOLOGRAPHIC ARTS

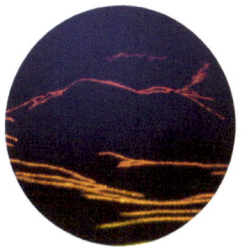

The exhibition *The Floating World* presents key transmission holograms by Rudie Berkhout. The exhibited works span 11 years from 1978 to 1989, representing the first phase of his career. Berkhout's experiments with holography began in 1975 after taking a class at the New York School of Holography. During a residency at Brown University in 1976 he developed an image and color multiplication technique that is the basis of his transmission work. This technique where light is controlled with holographic optical elements was revisited in 1978 to create compositions such as *12mW Boogie*, a pivotal artwork. Berkhout continued to produce groundbreaking holographic works and exhibitions until his death in 2008.

Berkhout was a sculptor of light, casting shapes with lenses, translucent materials, and holographic optical elements. The artist used holograms to catch and replay patterns and forms to compose scenes with depth and spatial dynamics. He wrote: "By experimenting, I 'ask' the medium what its unique qualities are. The imagery that unfolds are transformations of light through a variety of lenses, including holographic ones. I isolate light patterns, movement and/or shapes and arrange them in real or virtual holographic space."[1] Viewing one of Berkhout's transmission holograms is a visual engagement with another world. Space is created purely of light and made animate by the motion of viewing. The viewer moves around to play the hologram and becomes aware of his or her own perception. The act of looking is entangled with the scene composed in light. To float optical sculptures in holograms, Berkhout mastered holography to articulate shapes and space in a way that no one had done before. His visual style is distinctive and crisp.

WHAT IS A HOLOGRAM?

"A hologram is a three dimensional picture made with laser light."
– Rudie Berkhout[2]

Optical holography was theorized and then developed by scientists, with transmission holography and reflection holography arising independently from different fields of inquiry.[3] Dennis Gabor proposed the theory of holographic imaging in 1948 but it was only after the invention of the laser in 1960 that holographic imaging became feasible. The full potential of the technique became apparent in 1964 when Juris Leith and Emmett Upatnieks created the first off-axis transmission holograms (enabling the viewer to look at the image without the illuminating light getting in the way) and Yuri Denisyuk produced the first reflection holograms.

Holograms have a magic—we look at a surface and perceive space. This expansion of the image into the third dimension allows new expressive forms to be communicated. Depth and shape are captured by the hologram because the whole wavefront—the shape and direction—of light is recorded and reconstructed.

Laser light is used to record holograms because it is a single coherent wavelength—the waves of light are identical, with the same length between peaks and all peaks are in sync. This produces a pure spectral color, such at the red light from a Helium-Neon laser with a wavelength of 632 nanometers. A laser simultaneously illuminates a scene and is shone directly onto the holographic film as a reference beam. The waves of light from the object and the reference beam meet, adding together and canceling each other out, to create an interference pattern that encodes both beams. A holography set-up is usually a tabletop layout of optics that are arranged to illuminate a scene and record it into a holographic image. The laser beam is split, expanded, and shaped to illuminate both the scene and the holographic plate or film.

The hologram is a recording of the interference pattern into photosensitive film. To be recorded the interference pattern needs to be stable for the duration of the exposure which can be several minutes. This means eliminating all movement in the hologram set-up, which is done by isolating the equipment from vibrations.[4] When illuminating a laser transmission hologram the reconstructed scene appears exactly as it was recorded. The hologram is a like a window that can record and reconstruct light passing through it [**Fig. 1–3**].

A hologram captures a plane of perspective—a virtual window that records and replays the scene. The larger the hologram the more the viewer can peer around, allowing for depth information and an extended perspective of the scene. By contrast, a pinhole camera casts an image by spreading out light to produce an image from a single point perspective. The photographic image captures a one-point perspective that is recorded onto a plane. The hologram captures an area of perspective to reconstruct a volume. Our eyes are only small apertures from which the scene in front of us is perceived, therefore when viewing a hologram we can look into and around the recorded scene.

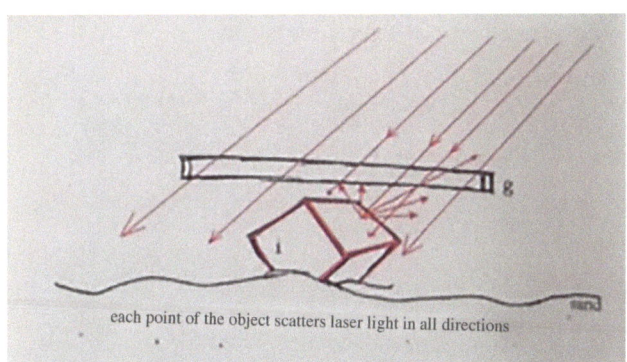

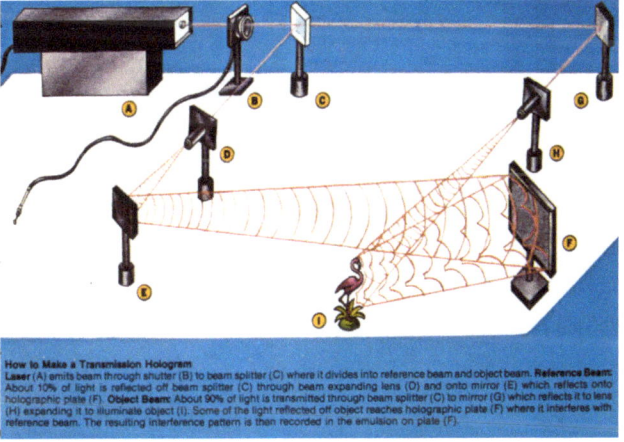

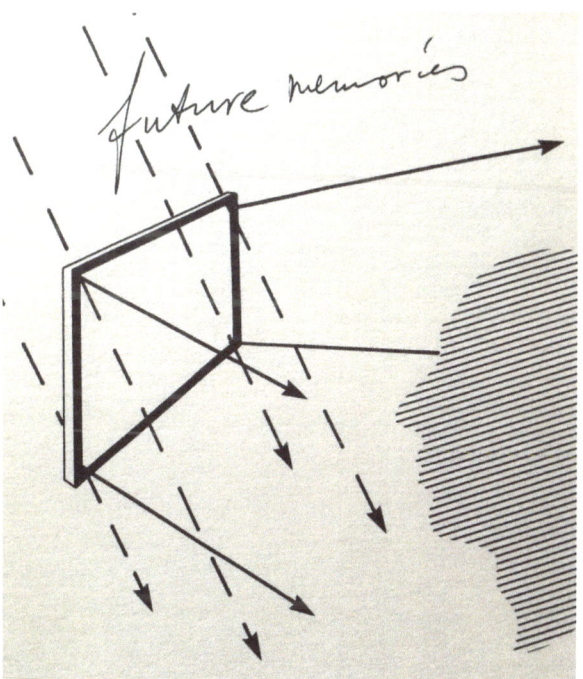

Fig. 1 Rudie Berkhout. Diagram of recoding a reflection hologram of a cube (i) into a hologram (g) "each point of the object scatters laser light in all directions," in *Holography: An Introduction to Bending Light*, 2005. Courtesy Rudie Berkhout Estate.
Fig. 2 Rudie Berkhout. Cover image of brochure for *Future Memories*, James Prendergast Library, 1983. Courtesy Rudie Berkhout Estate.
Fig. 3 Hudson Talbott and Rudie Berkhout. *How to Make a Transmission Hologram*, n.d. Courtesy Rudie Berkhout Estate.

SHAPES IN LIGHT

"A hologram is like a lens, bending the light that
shines through it, shaping the light so that the viewer
can see an image in three dimensions."
– Rudie Berkhout [5]

Berkhout worked with holography but described the medium as "light itself."[6] With *Photon Study #10* (1978) an array of dots fills the composition [**Plate 1**]. Berkhout poses the holographic space as a field of light. At this time holograms were mostly of three-dimensional scenes, still-lives, and miniature dioramas built out of sturdy materials and rendered into holographic images. In comparison, *Photon Study #10* and his subsequent works seem to float in space. While creating these fields of light, Berkhout also reveals his technique by showing the edges of the transparent sheets from which the light points are formed. It is as if he wants us to see into and appreciate the construction of the holographic image.

Produced in 1978, *12mW Boogie* propelled Berkhout to the attention of the art community [**Plate 2**]. This three-panel hologram is composed of shapes, clusters, and arrays of elements with distinct colors, which are animated as the viewer moves. To create optical objects for his holograms Berkhout experimented with structured glass, diffusers, and baffles such as the "cube" in *12mW Boogie* made from three panels of diffusing glass [**Fig. 4**]. *12mW Boogie* was the first hologram Berkhout completed using the technique of multiplying optical shapes with holographic optical elements (HOEs). Master holograms were multiplied in space and color-space using two HOEs. These techniques of color control and image multiplication became a signature of Berkhout's transmission holograms.

"I began with one cube and two spheres, which were recorded in three
separate master holograms. With the help of a Holographic Optical
Element (HOE) that I designed especially for this task, I made many cubes
and spheres from the original masters in multiple colors. It was the first time
that I used several HOE's in the image making process of a finished work."
– Rudie Berkhout [7]

Berkhout explored how holograms can shape and direct light and created holograms not only to record objects but also to be windows that would transform the light coming through them. These holographic optical elements can be made to split, spread, and reshape light. For example if three point light sources are recorded with a reference beam into a hologram then three beams will emerge when that hologram is replayed. Where this becomes interesting is if the light passing through this holographic optical element is an image, say a cube, then three cubes will be projected. A holographic optical element transforms light. Mathematically this type of transformation is called a Fourier synthesis, and can be used to calculate the waveform produced by combining sinusoidal waves or signals. In music, notes of different wavelengths combine as Fourier synthesis to produce a chord.

The holographic optical element reshapes and divides the wavefront of light. Adding together master images with holographic optical elements, or combining holographic optical elements, results in the multiplication of visual forms [**Fig. 6**]. Berkhout continued experimenting with this technique and created holograms such

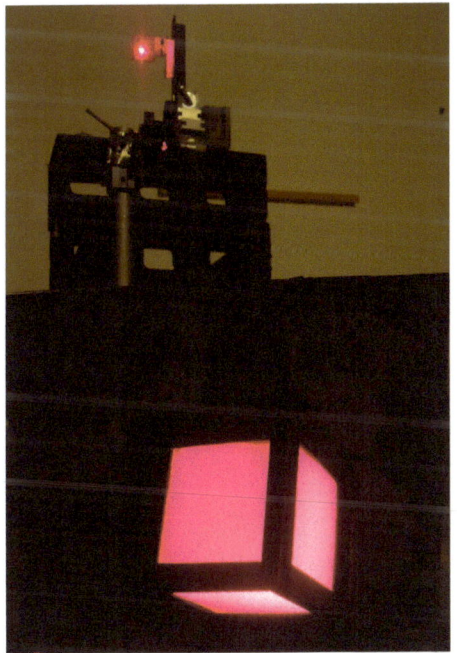

as the "Spatial Frequency" series in 1979, where simple visual elements were optically multiplied. He also created laser "star" projectors from holographic optical elements that sprayed a field of light lines from a single beam.

With *Event Horizon* (1980) [**Plate 5**] Berkhout first created a visual element directly from light. The dynamic spiral element around the central sphere in *Event Horizon*—what Berkhout called the "moving energy"—was produced by recording "light itself."[8] This dynamic visual element was produced using a large imperfect lens and two holographic optical elements. The HOEs multiplied and extended the focused light of the lens to "smear" into a spatially dynamic shape.[9] Two holographic optical elements were produced and combined to create the "moving energy" in *Event Horizon* [**Fig. 7–9**].[10]

Fig. 4 Optical cube made from diffusers and cardboard baffles. Photograph by Martina Mrongovius in Berkhout's studio, 2015.

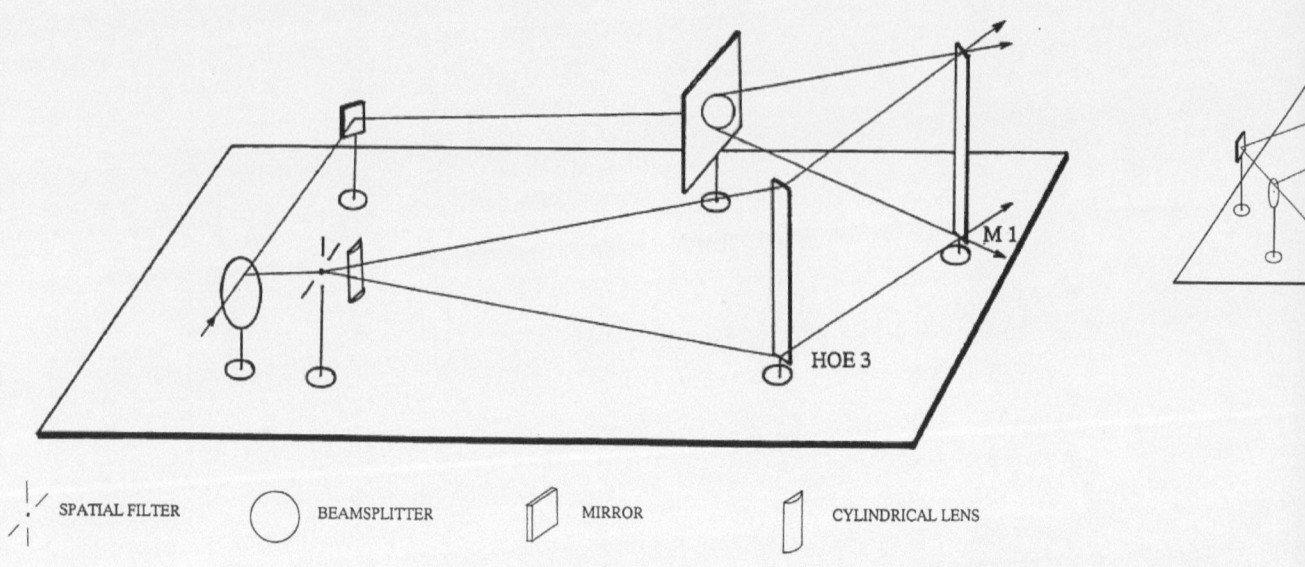

SPATIAL FILTER   BEAMSPLITTER   MIRROR   CYLINDRICAL LENS

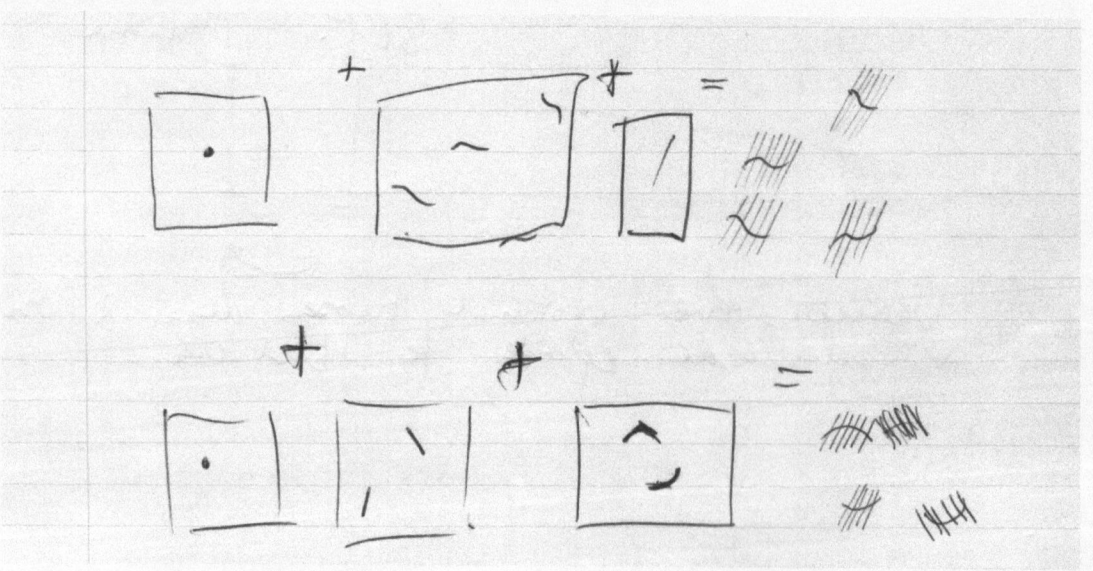

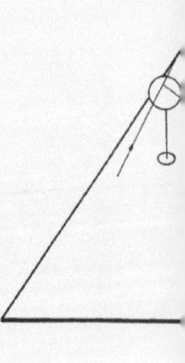

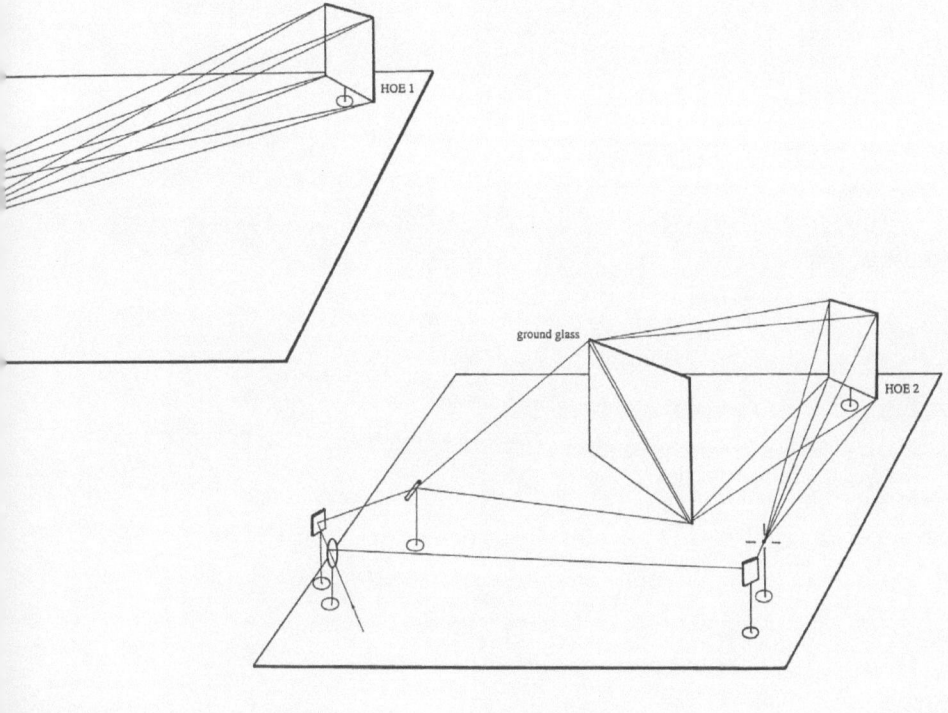

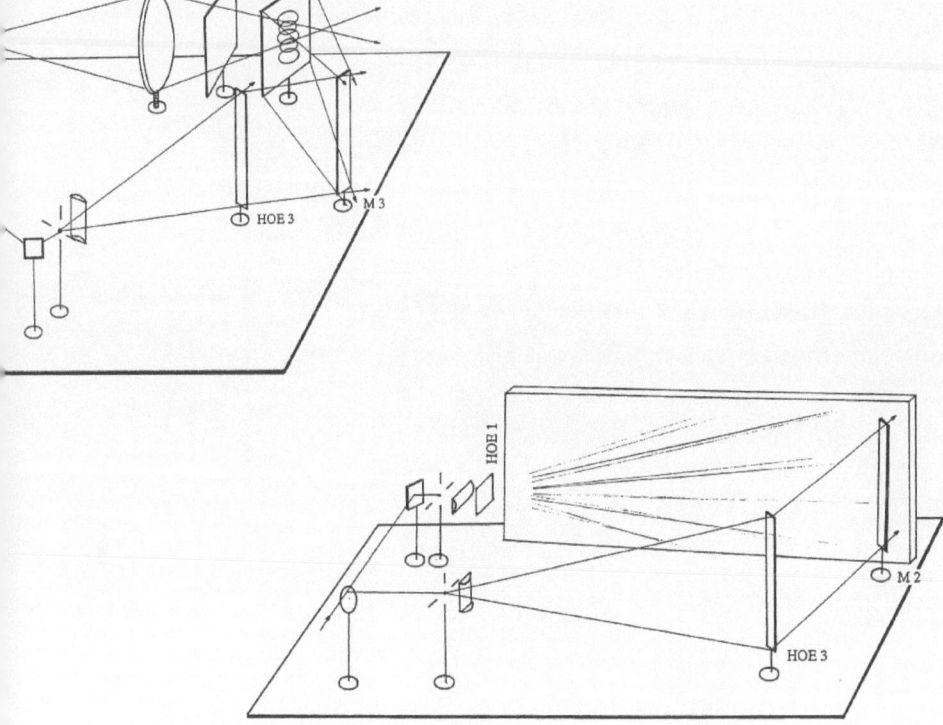

COLOR IN HOLOGRAPHIC SPACE

"Recording several master holograms on one white light transmission hologram makes multiple color compositions possible."
– Rudie Berkhout [11]

Color control was another key aspect of Berkhout's work. Transmission holograms when replayed with white light produce a rainbow of colors. Stand in front of one of Berkhout's transmission holograms, move up and down and see the colors change. You are moving through an expanded spectrum of light. Berkhout's holograms however do not have a "rainbow" appearance. Berkhout used strip masters to place each image element and create a tuned spectral window. The position of the master holograms in relation to the final print creates viewing windows with different vertical spectrums. Red light bends[12] more than blue light creating a spectrum with the perceived color dependent on the recording geometry and the viewer's position.

Event Horizon was produced from three masters, "the sphere" M 1, "the field" M 2 and "moving energy" M 3 [**Fig. 5, 9, & 10**]. These three masters were combined with the transfer geometry shown in Berkhout's diagrams of table set-up and top-view [**Fig. 11–12**].[13] When the hologram is viewed each transferred holographic image element is a distinct color. This technique of combining colored elements was also used by Berkhout to create scenes with more neutral and pastel colors by replaying two masters to combine two overlaid shapes. By overlapping elements of spectral color the shapes combine to be the additive color. Using precise "achromatic" [14] geometry, colors can be mixed to make white. The central line element in *Break Even* (1989) has two colors that hover around each other, combining and breaking apart depending on the viewing position.

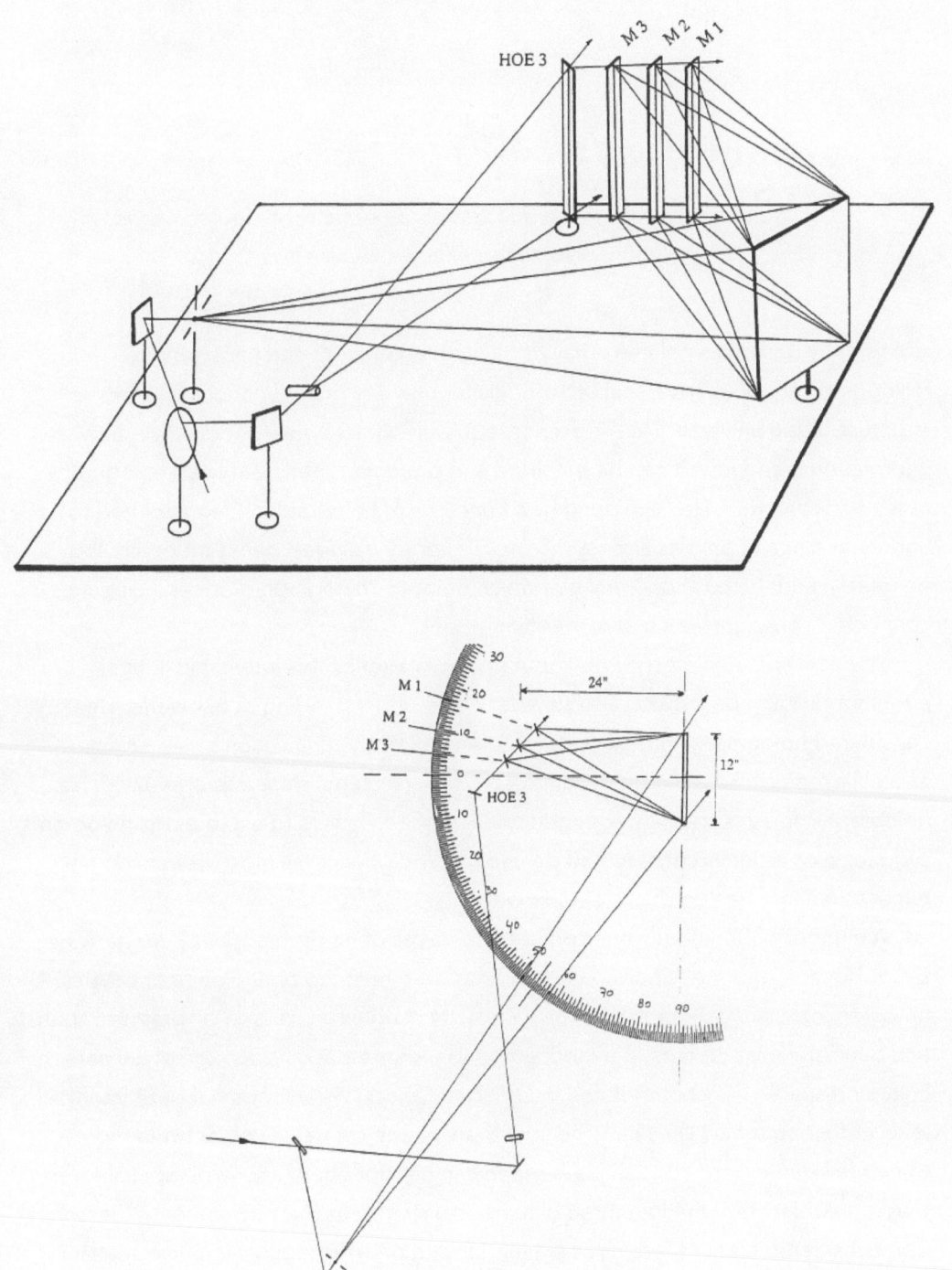

Fig. 11–12

Rudie Berkhout. Diagram of table set-up and top-view diagram of the transfer geometry for *Event Horizon*. Courtesy Rudie Berkhout Estate.

INTO THE FOURTH DIMENSION

*"I could develop the technique and at the same time create images
reaching previously unknown visual areas."*
– Rudie Berkhout [15]

Holography posed a whole new way of thinking about light and information.
Holographic theories have enabled models for how the brain functions and the
structure of the universe. Thinking holographically allows a new perspective on what
information is and how it can be enfolded and projected. Berkhout used holography
as a visual tool while also exploring how concepts of holographic theory related to
understandings of physics and mysticism. His library included books on psychology,
geometry, and the cosmos—many of which point to "holographic" ideas including
connected consciousness and higher dimensions.

The concepts explored by Berkhout in his work reflect his interest in light as
a tool for probing perception and developing an understanding of our world. He
considered holography to be a powerful medium for the unification of art, science,
and philosophy.[16] Fundamental and metaphysical concepts were expressed with his
holographic images spatially arranged to encourage viewers to explore. His holograms
produce a questioning of assumed perception and physics, as most viewers do not
expect that light can be shaped in this way.

A number of Berkhout's titles point to concepts of modern physics.[17] *Matterwave*,
Event Horizon, and the "Photon Study" series each relate to phenomena of physics. A
hologram's dynamic three-dimensional capacity enables expressive diagrams of spatial
and temporal relationships. Berkhout employs a shape-based language of animate
color and space. The central shape in *Enfolded Colors* (1991) draws our gaze into tracing
an ever-folding torus [**Fig. 13**].[18] The spatial animation creates an object with more
than three dimensions. This animate shape can be thought of as a hyperspatial form
that is unfolded into multiple three dimensional shapes as the viewer moves. Berkhout
also considered his installations as creating a kind of hyperspace—a fourth spatial
dimension created by the way optical objects extend out from the holographic plane.[19]

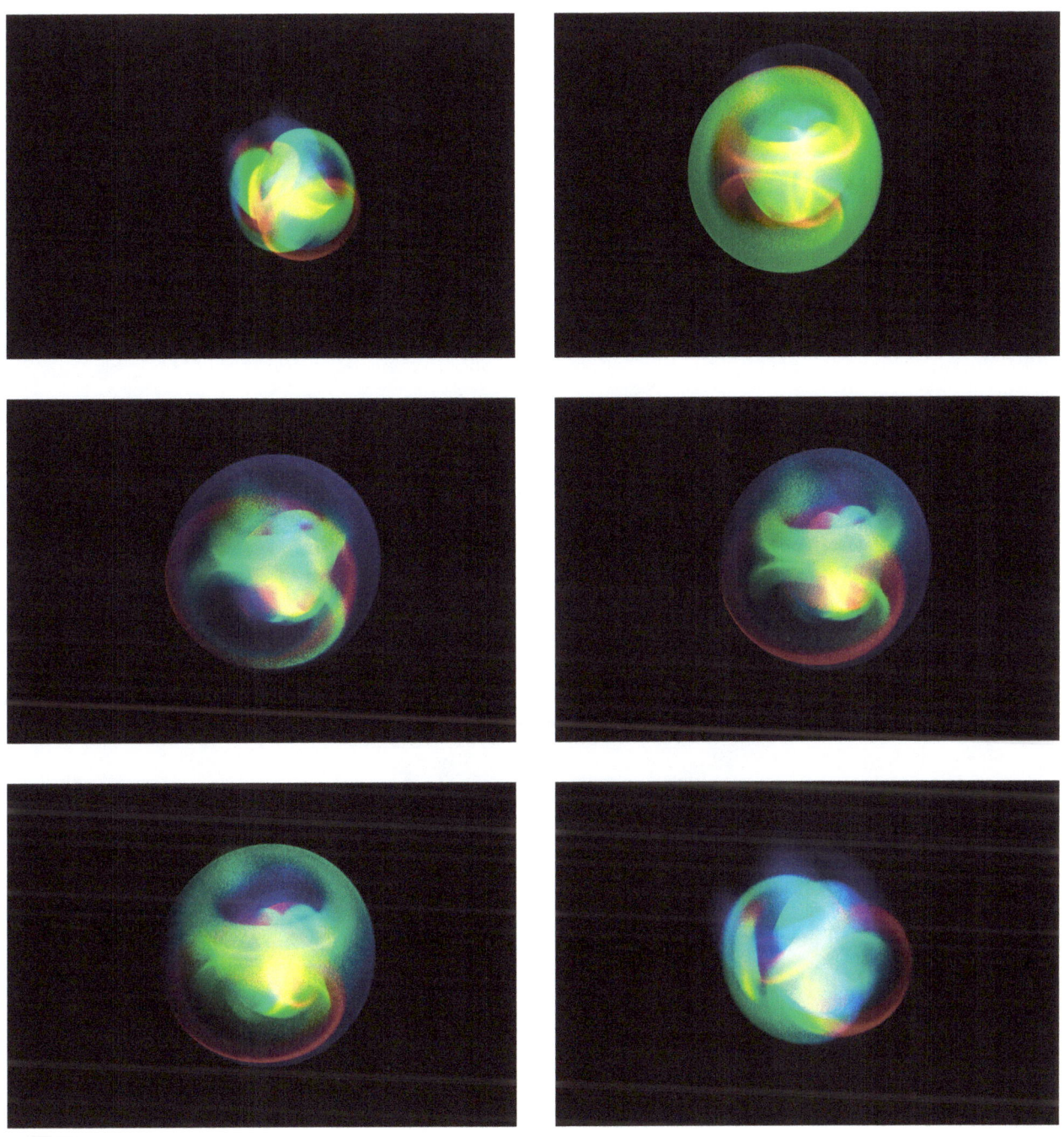

Fig. 13
Rudie Berkhout. Sequence of views of *Enfolded Colors*, 1991. Transmission hologram: silver-halide glass plate.
Courtesy Rudie Berkhout Estate.

CONSTRUCTION OF HOLOGRAPHIC SPACE

"The possibilities of working with high-tech outside the corporate
structure and using it as an art medium appealed to me."
– Rudie Berkhout [20]

Berkhout built studios and his own holographic printing set-ups to craft these holographic scenes. His holographic laboratories enabled the precise control of light with handmade components. There was a harmonious order to Berkhout's arrangement of space and equipment. "I see technology as an integral part of nature and my function being to articulate its beauty," he said.[21] Custom-built parts are used together to shape light. Berkhout worked on a sand table to provide the stability required for hologram recording at his studio in Manhattan. He also sculpted and recorded the surface of the sand into his compositions. Sculpting sand allowed him to shape surfaces and lines. Planes of light were traced into holographic images from the contours of the sand table.

The New Territories (1984) [**Plate 10**] is a diptych that creates a deep landscape of backlit ridges, transferred with distinct colors of dramatic evening light. The title refers to Berkhout's exploration and then move to the Hudson Valley where he built a home and studio with a view of the Catskill Mountains. The view to the mountains is recreated in the sculpted sand ridges which Berkhout recorded into the hologram at his Manhattan studio.

The house and studio Berkhout built in the Catskills feels like an extension of his craftsmanship, a viewing platform from which to watch nature's play of light. After his move upstate his works became more concerned with natural phenomena. He turned his attention to creating reflection holograms and recorded the patterns that emerge from mixtures of liquid and light. In these reflection works optical phenomena are captured to create artworks where light is both the medium and the subject. In addition to his holographic prints Berkhout created holographic optical elements that were included in star projectors and arranged for installations to produce fields and sprays of projected light. Berkhout also experimented with outdoor installations and stereo photography of the landscape.

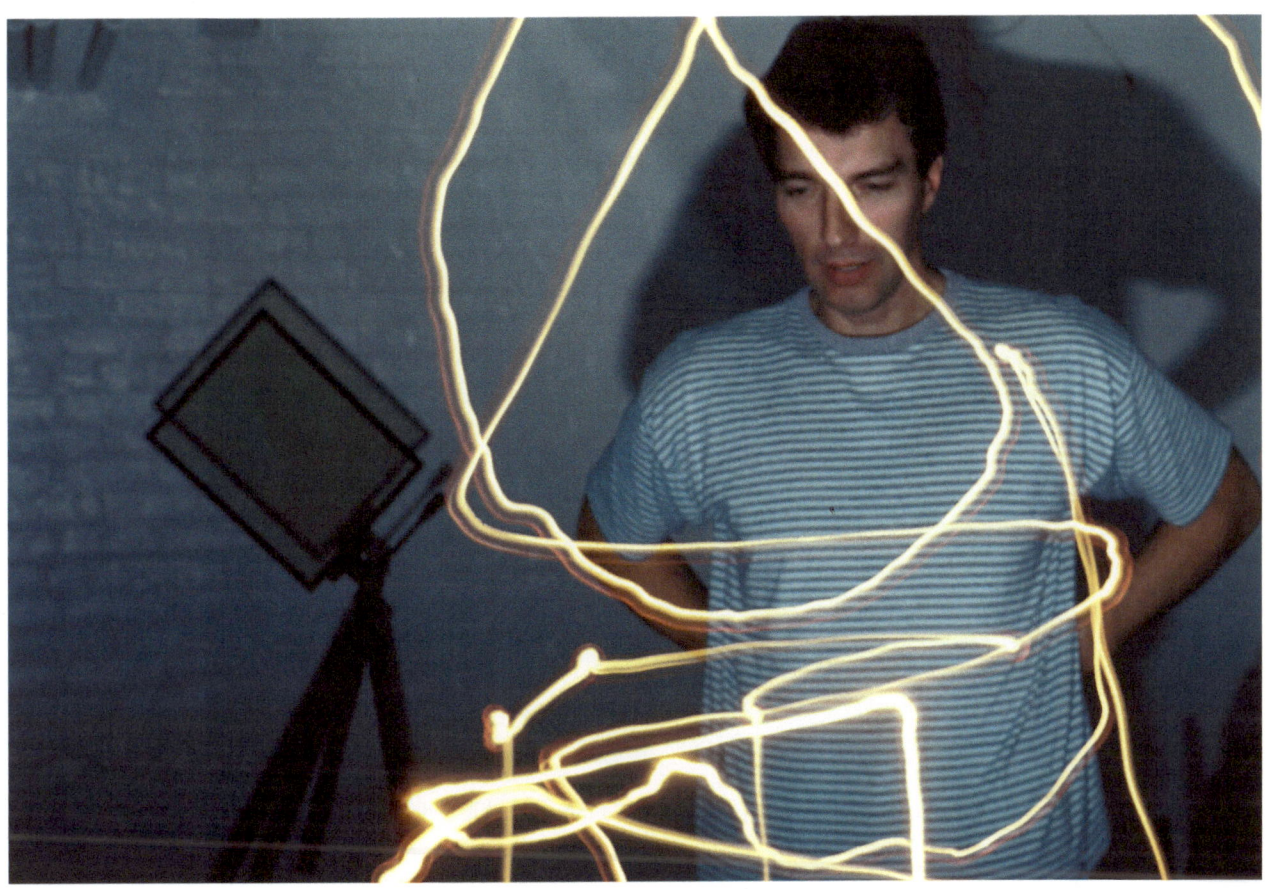

Rudie Berkhout playing with light, 1985. Courtesy Rudie Berkhout Estate.

The works in *The Floating World* show Berkhout's mastery of the holographic medium. Berkhout was a bender of light, casting shapes with lenses, translucent materials, and holographic optical elements. The artist used holograms to catch and replay patterns and forms. The pure line of the laser was expanded and shaped. Master holograms and holographic optical elements were combined to create new compositions. Berkhout meticulously designed the color, placement, and viewing dynamics to create new scenes of imaginary landscapes.

Rudie Berkhout was also a teacher and believed, "holography is a new technique that can be explored and developed further by everybody."[22] Berkhout's own practice brought holography to a new level of design. Each hologram has a mysterious beauty while evoking pure visual forms. The shapes, patterns, and rhythms he created in and with light are invitations to explore our own concepts of perception. Engaging with his holograms we become aware of our perceptions as we are enchanted with the holographic form.

Notes

1. Artist statement from leaflet *Painting with Light*, produced in conjunction with the installation *Odyssey 2001*.

2. Rudie Berkhout, *An Explanation of Holography*, self-published booklet, New York, 1983, 2. Emphasis his.

3. Gabor wanted to improve the resolution of the electron microscope, Leith and Upatnieks were working on side reading radar, and Denisyuk's holograms are an extension of Lippmann's integral "light field" photography and the Daguerreotype process.

4. Techniques to create a vibration-free environment include floating a heavy table on a cushion of air, working on a sand table, stopping/watching traffic, turning off air conditioning, and holding still.

5. Berkhout, *An Explanation of Holography*, 2.

6. Included in multiple artist statements including Berkhout, *Painting with Light*, 2001.

7. Rudie Berkhout, *12mW Boogie*, MIT Museum holography collection MOH-1978.06 online. https://webmuseum.mit.edu/detail.php?term=berkhout&module=objects&type=keyword&x=0&y=0&kv=67145&record=4&module=objects

8. Rudie Berkhout, *Investigating the Use of HOE's in the Holographic Image Making Process*, SPIE proceedings 2652, Practical Holography X (25 March 1996).

9. Ibid.

10. The *Event Horizon* diagrams were drawn by Rudie Berkhout and published in ibid.

11. Berkhout, *An Explanation of Holography*, 11.

12. Light "bends" and the spectrum is spread out because of the microstructure of the interference pattern. This bending of light is called diffraction.

13. See note 10.

14. Literally "without color," achromatic images are grayscale. In holography achromatic images add together hues to produce white light.

15. Rudie Berkhout, *The Holograms of Rudie Berkhout*, Fukuoka, Japan: Fukuoka Art Museum, 1988.

16. Rudie Berkhout, "Unifying Science and Art," in *New Spaces: The Holographer's Vision*, Philadelphia: The Franklin Institute Press, 1979. See page 13 in this catalogue for the full version.

17. "Modern physics" refers to theories of quantum mechanics and relativity developed since the 1890s including wave-particle duality and a model of the universe that includes black holes and gravitational lensing.

18. " 'Torus' is a mathematical word for donut." Rudolf v. B. Rucker, *Geometry, Relativity and the Fourth Dimension* (Mineola, NY: Dover Publications, 1977), 105. Berkhout kept this book in his library.

19. Berkhout, *Investigating The Use of HOE's in the Holographic Image Making Process*.

20. Berkhout, *The Holograms of Rudie Berkhout*, Fukuoka, 1988.

21. Berkhout, "Unifying Science and Art."

22. Berkhout, *An Explanation of Holography*, 2.

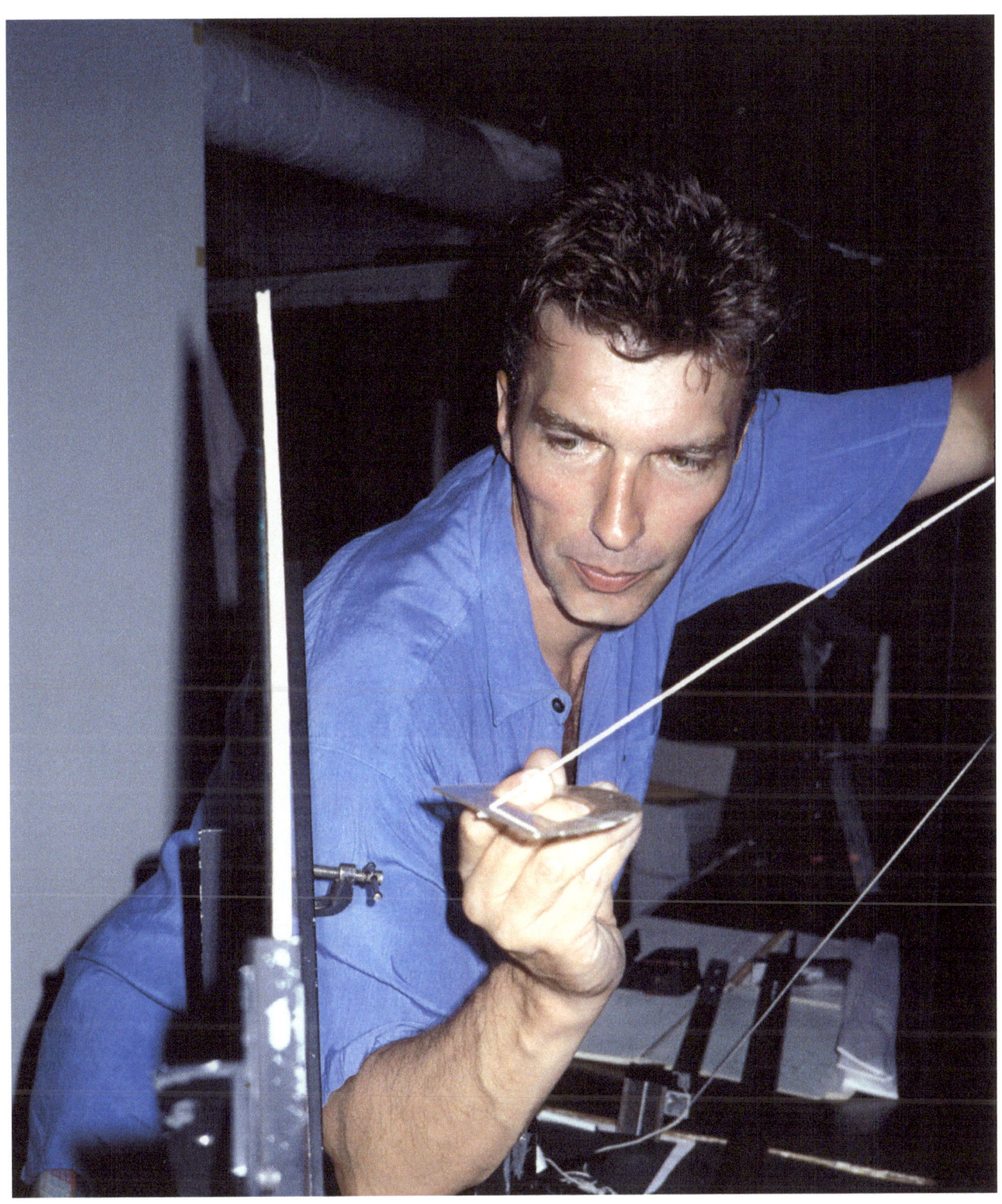

Rudie Berkhout, 1988. Courtesy Rudie Berkhout Estate.

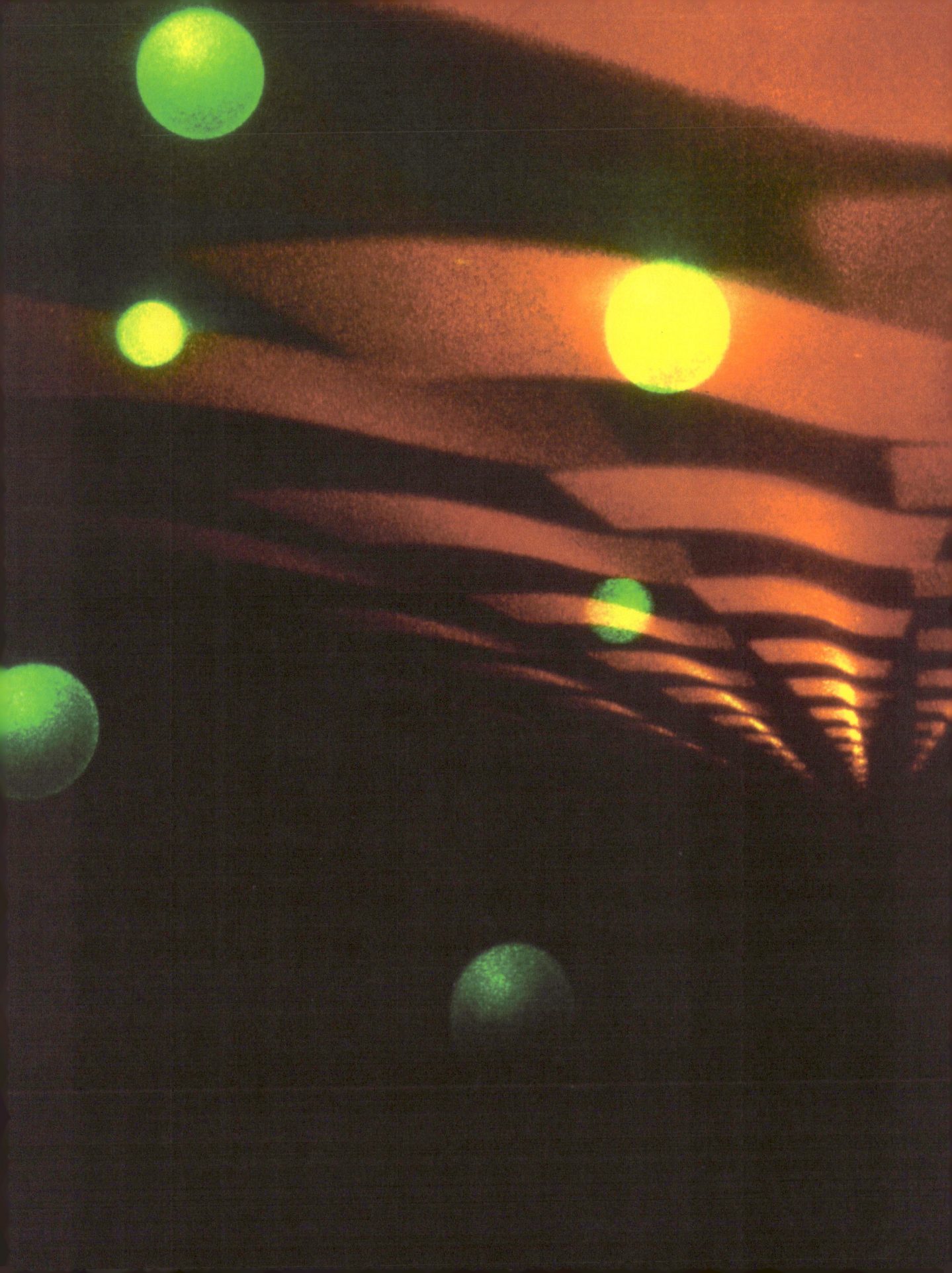

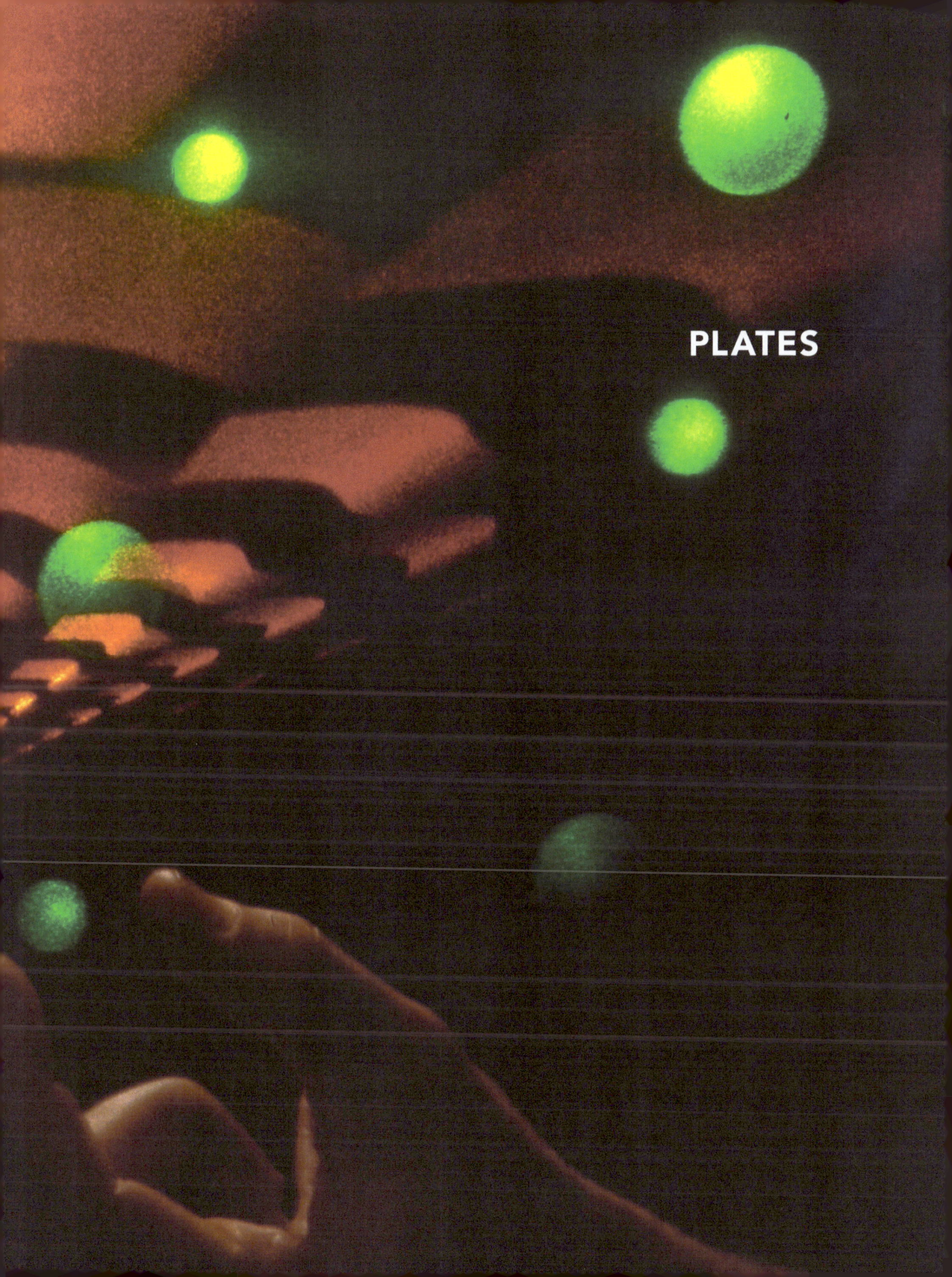

PLATES

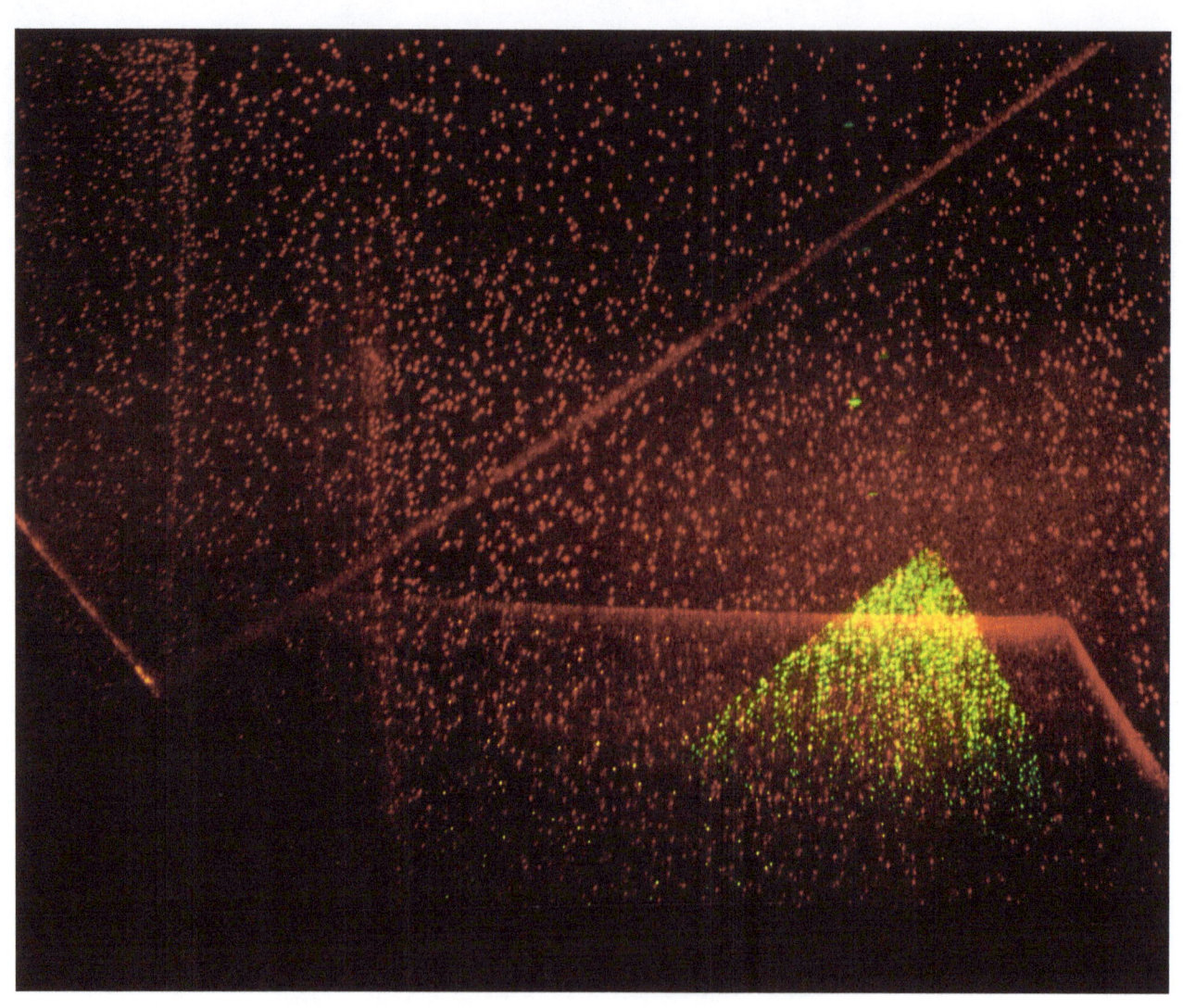

Plate 1

Photon Study #10, 1978

Transmission hologram: silver-halide glass plate

8 x 10 in., 12 x 16 in. overall

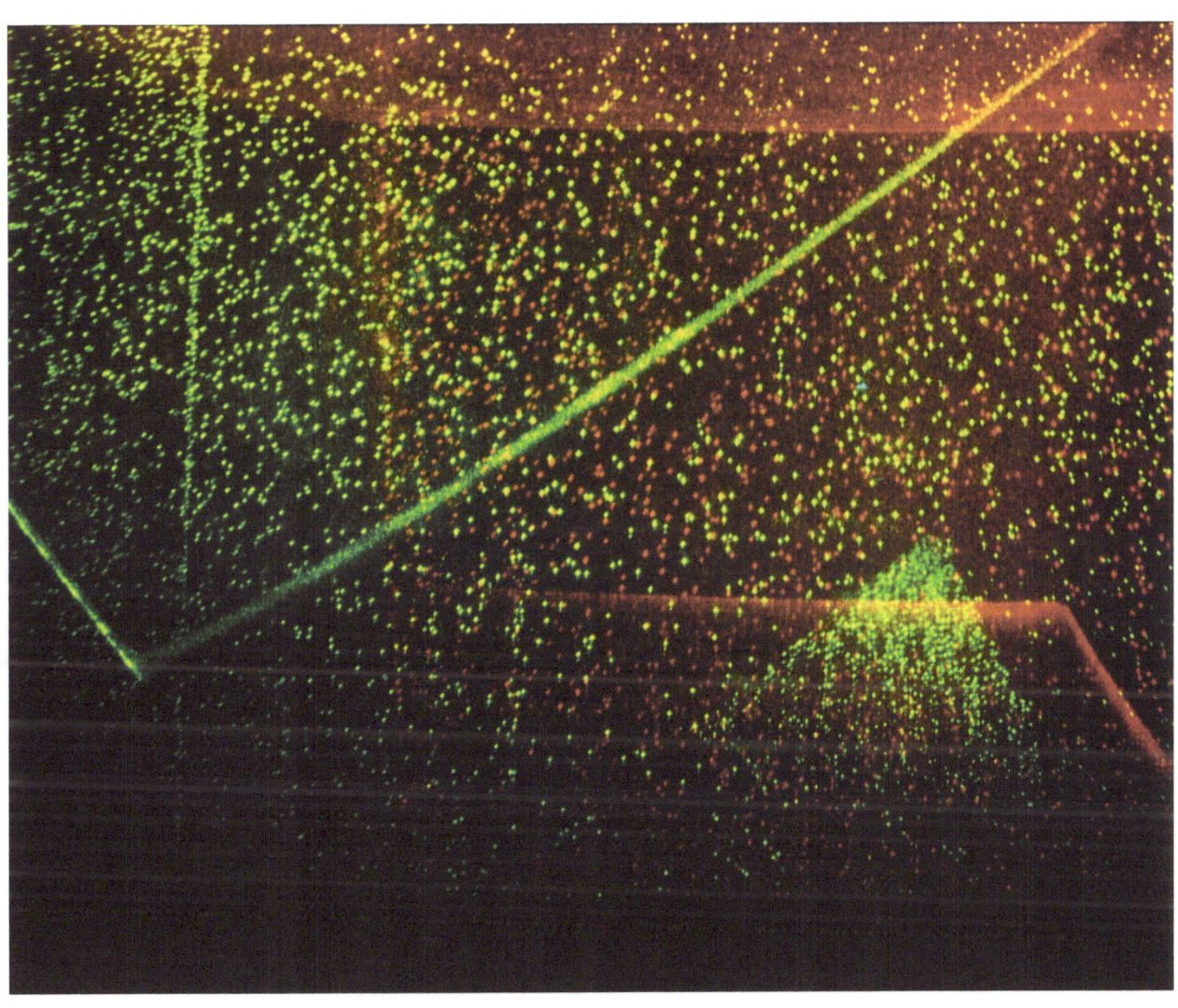

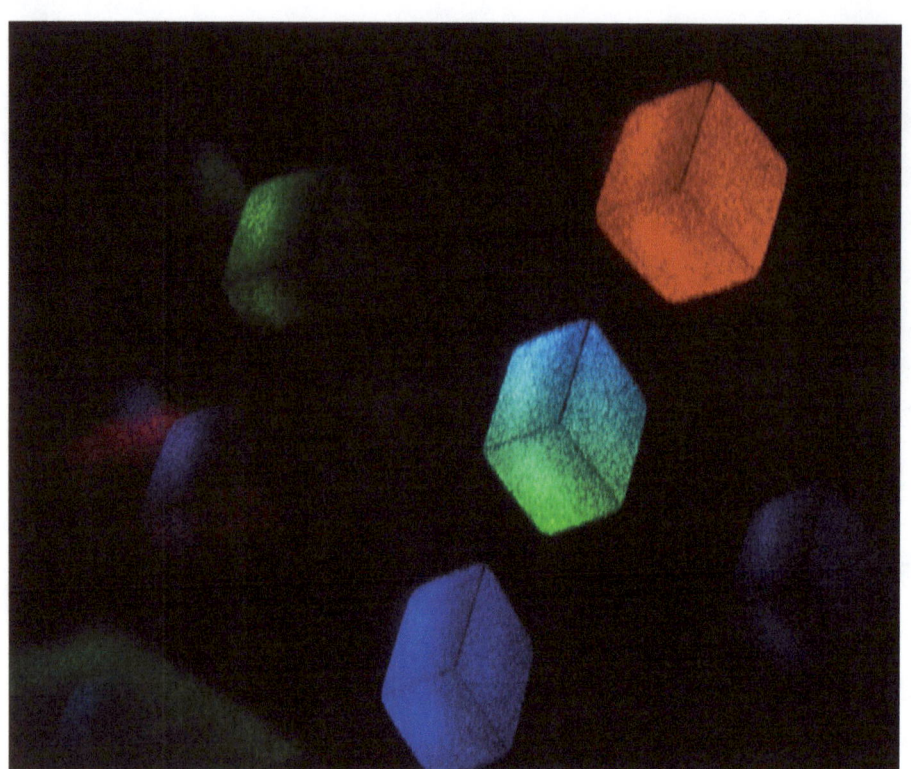
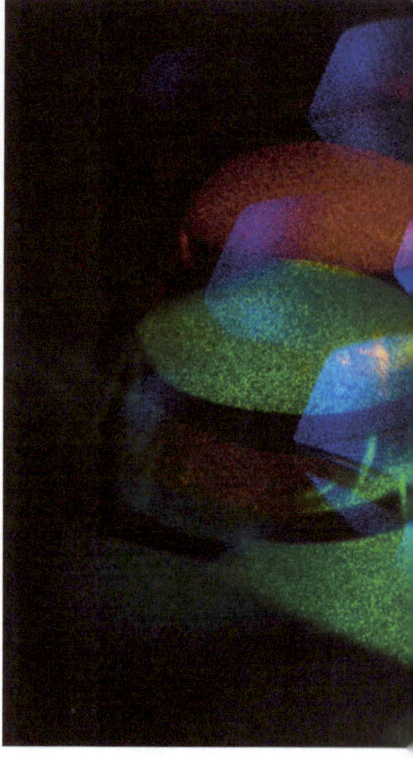

Plate 2

12mW Boogie, 1978
Transmission hologram: silver-halide glass plate; wood frame
Three parts, each 8 x 10 in.

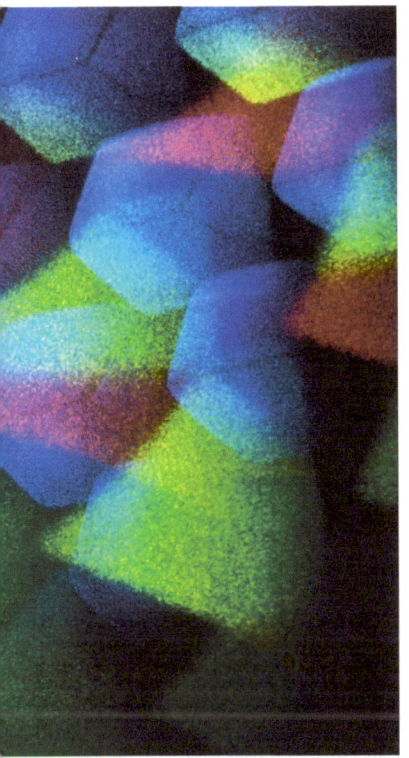

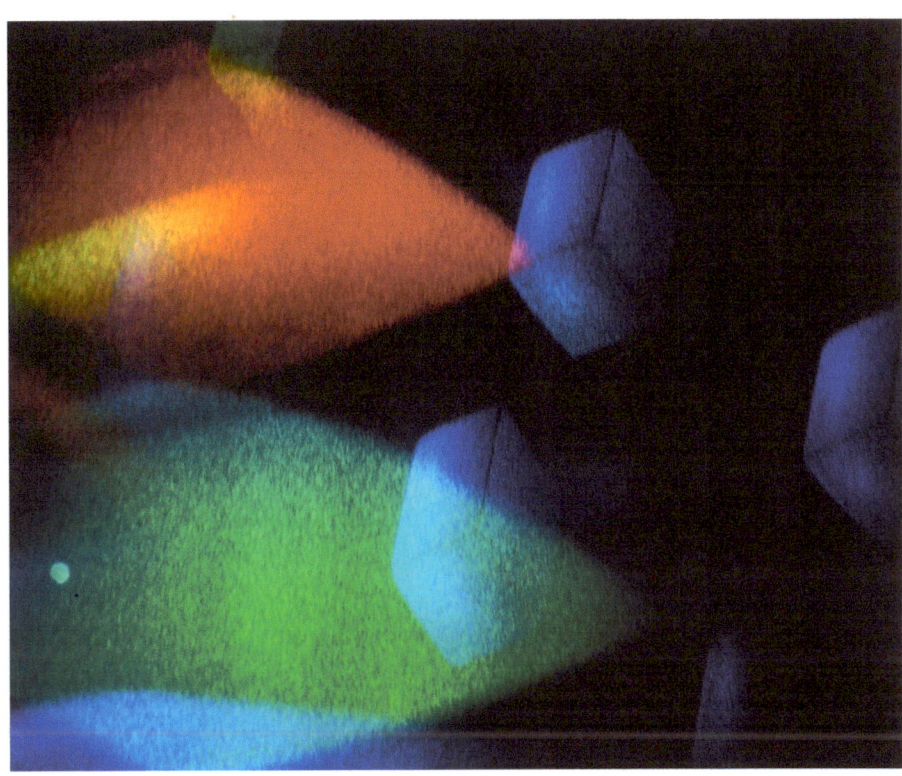

Plate 3

Future Memories, 1979

Transmission hologram: silver-halide glass plate

8 x 10 in., 12 x 16 in. overall

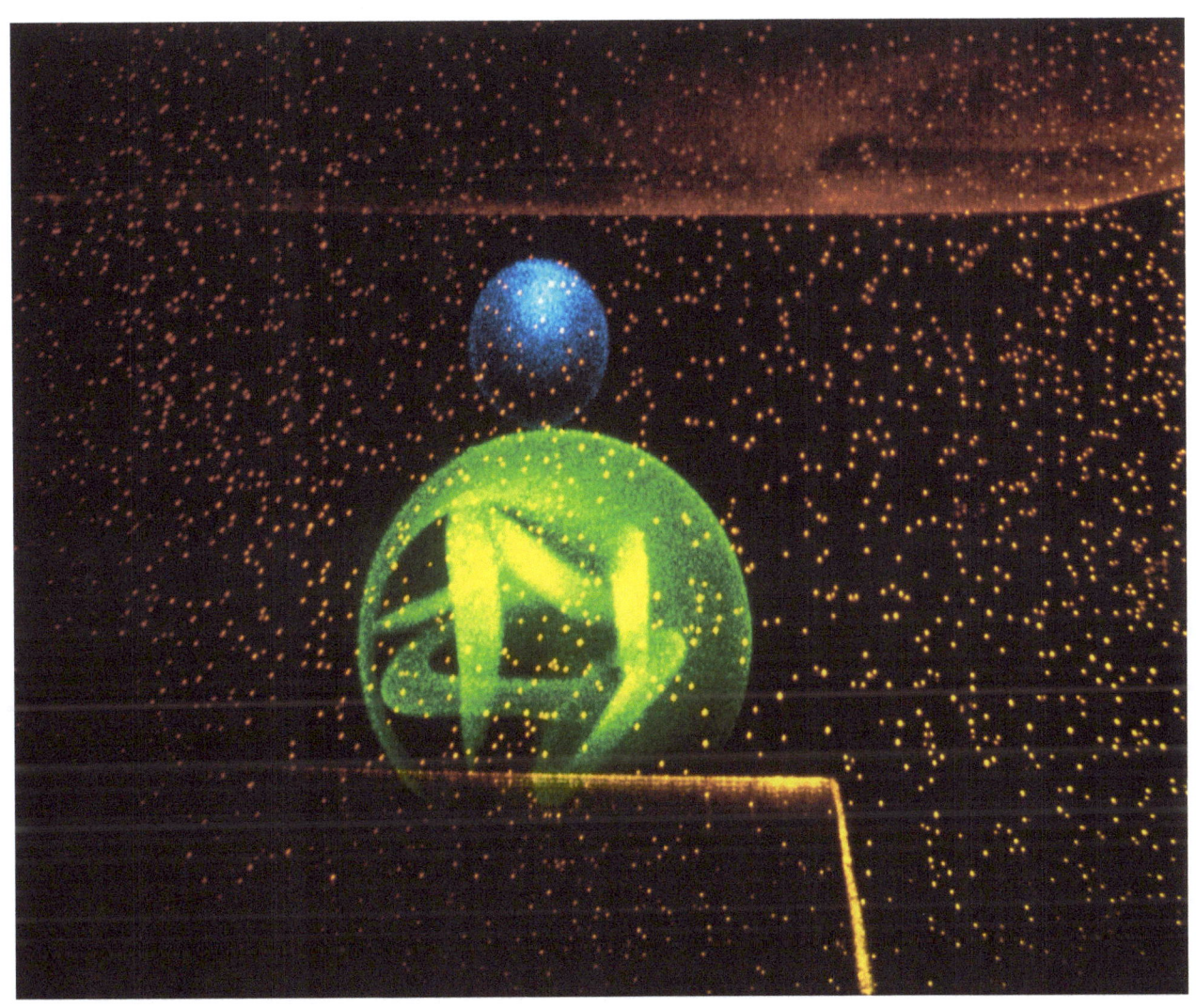

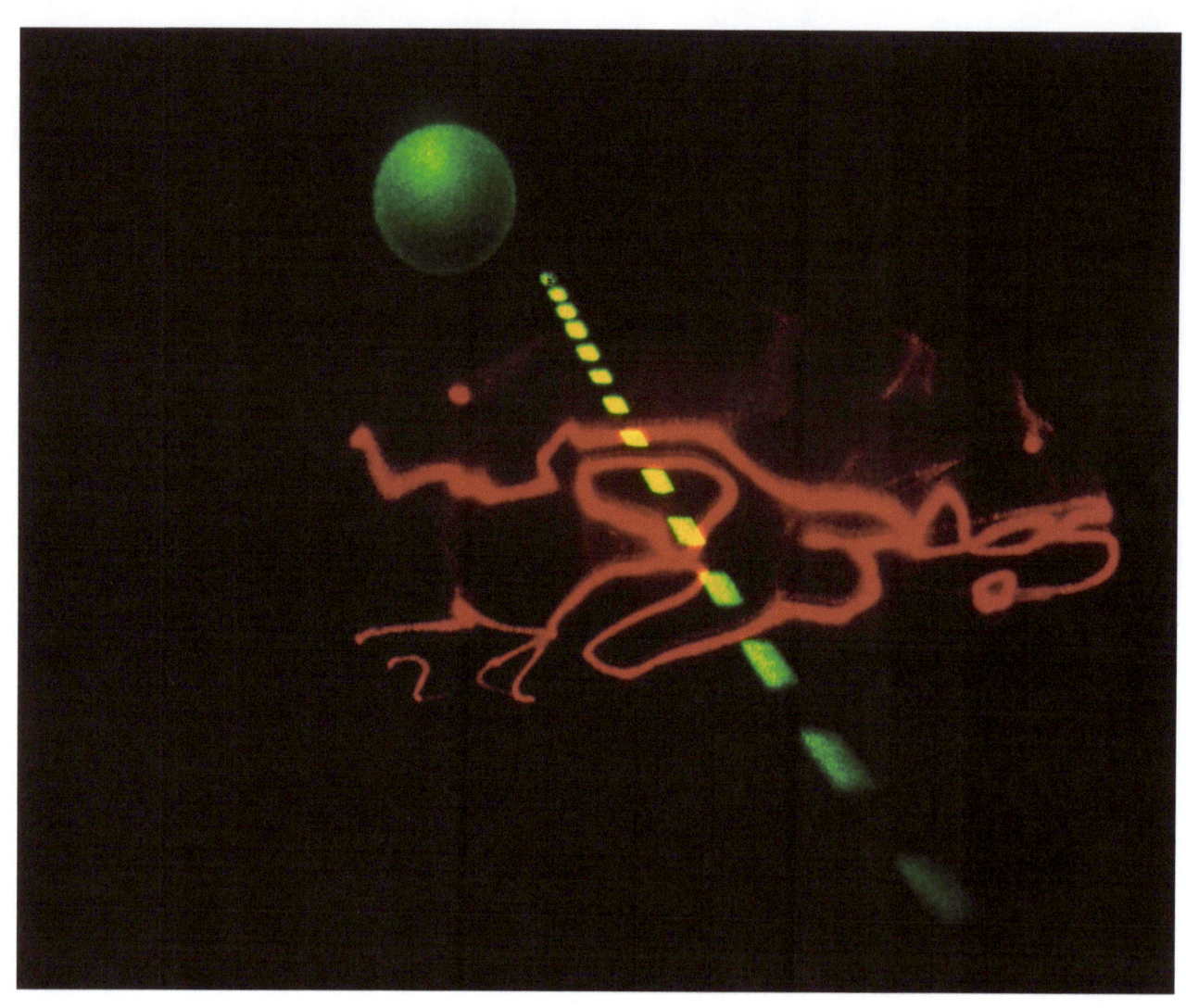

Plate 4

Transfer 137, 1980

Transmission hologram: silver-halide glass plate

8 x 10 in., 12 x 16 in. overall

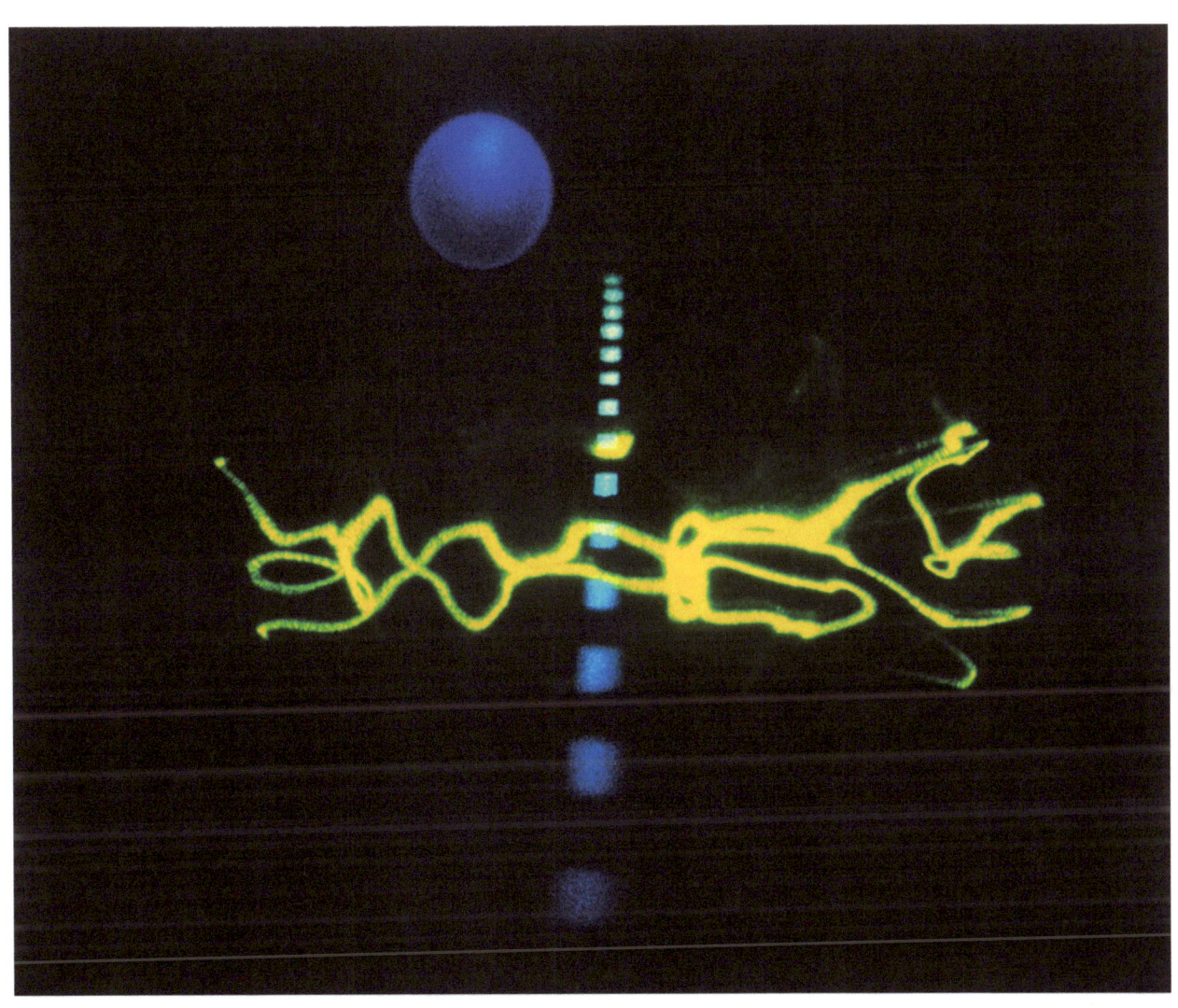

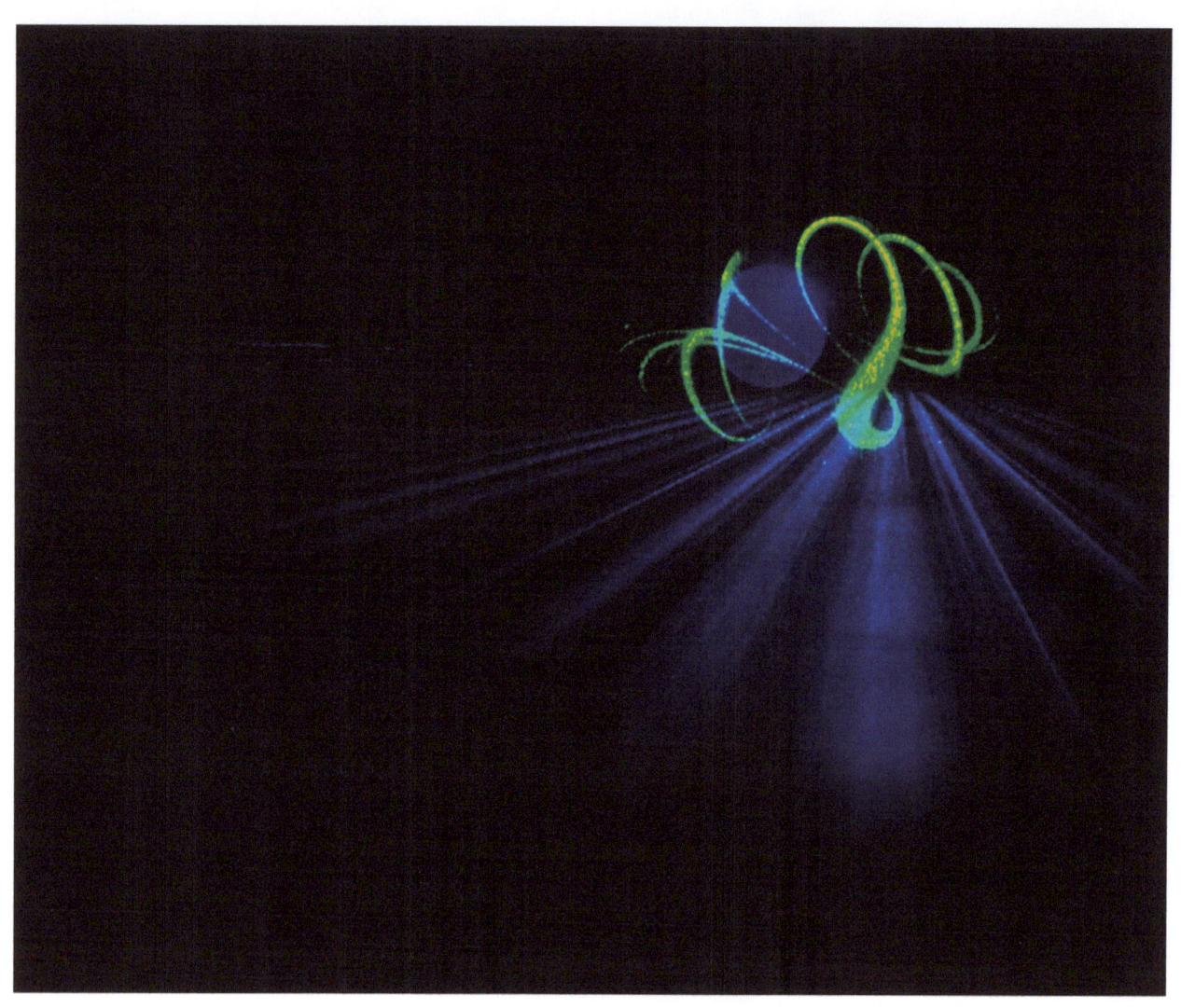

Plate 5

Event Horizon, 1980

Transmission hologram: silver-halide glass plate

8 x 10 in., 12 x 16 in. overall

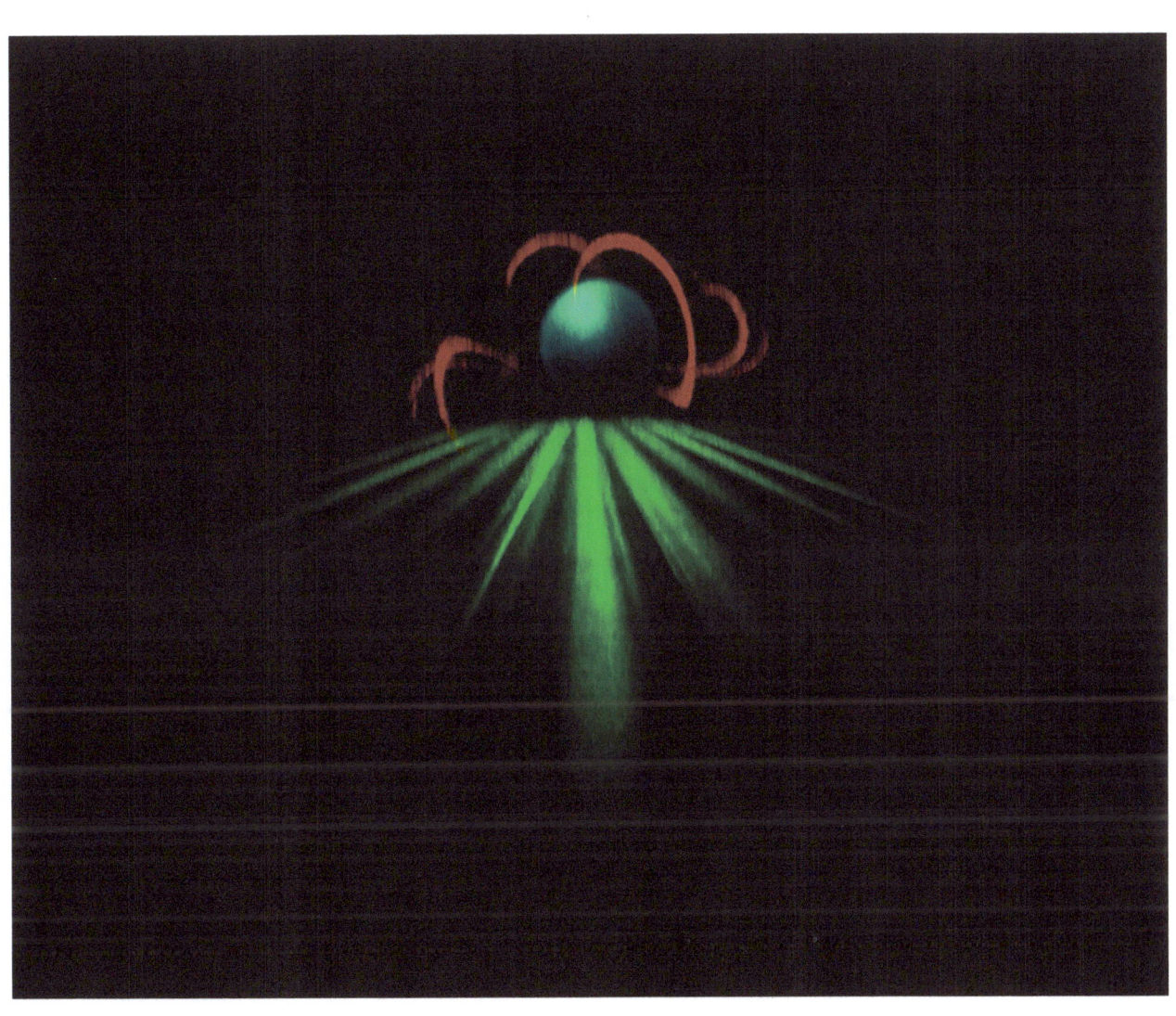

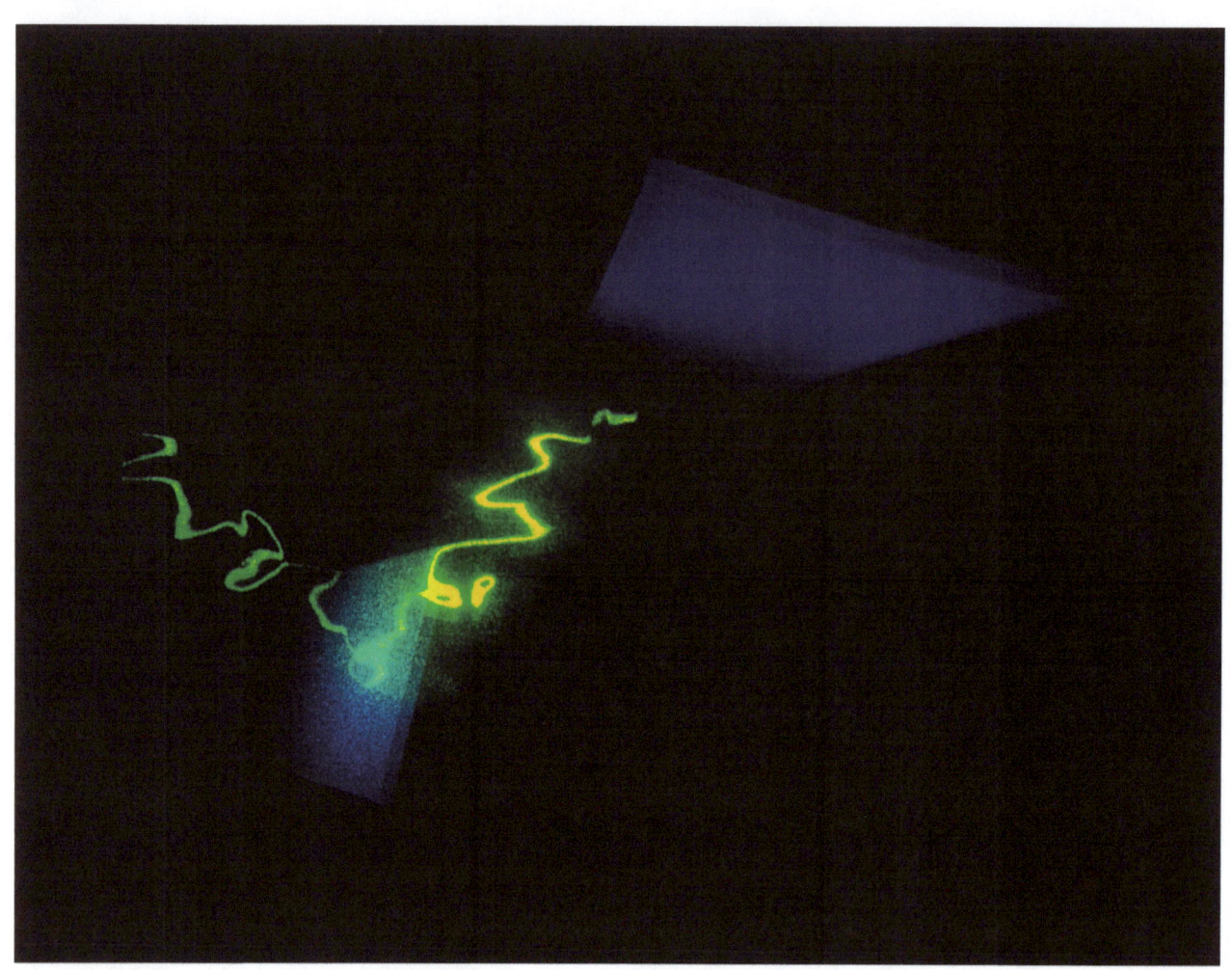

Plate 6

Ukiyo, 1981

Transmission hologram: silver-halide glass plate

12 x 16 in.

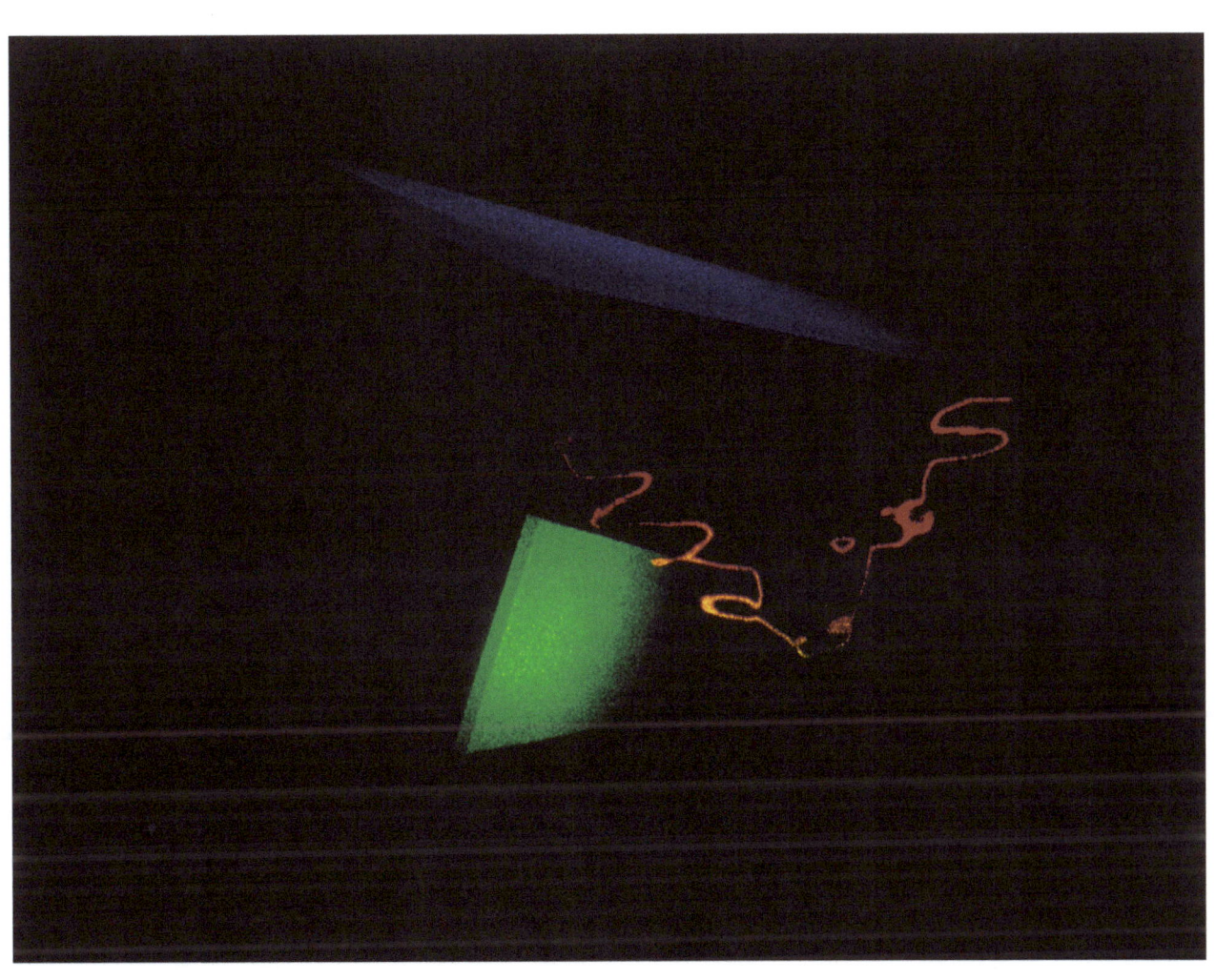

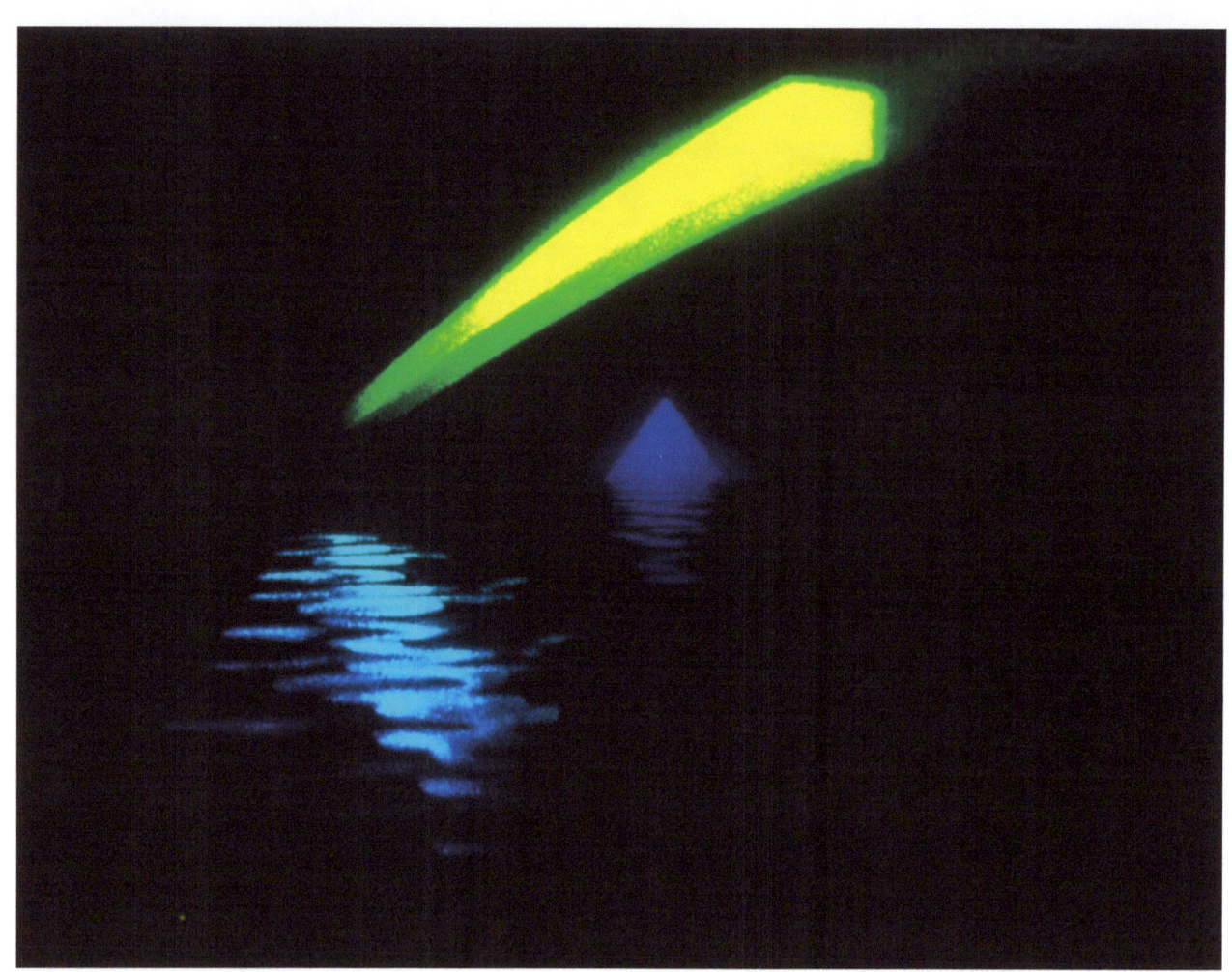

Plate 7

Toba, 1981

Transmission hologram: silver-halide glass plate

12 x 16 in.

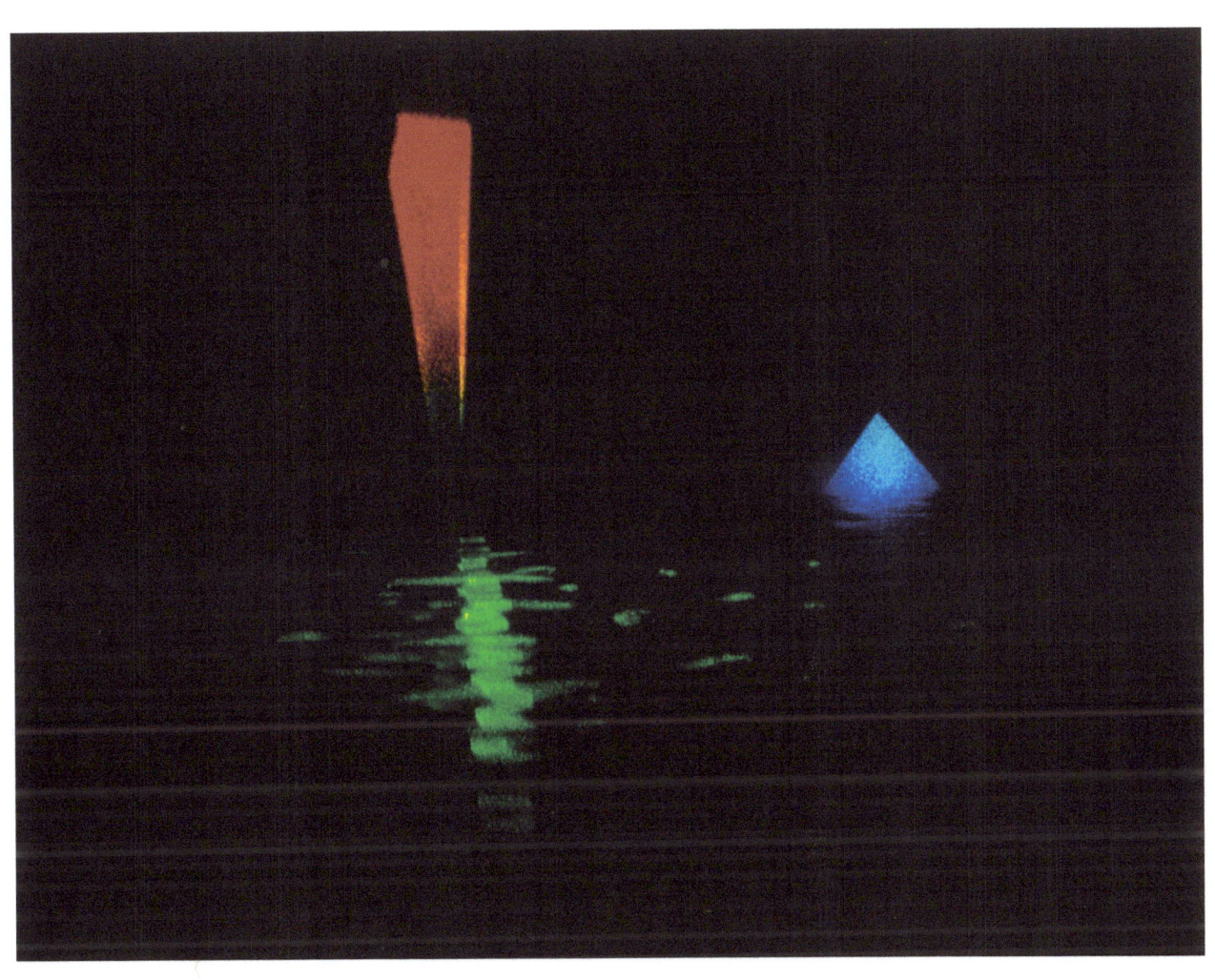

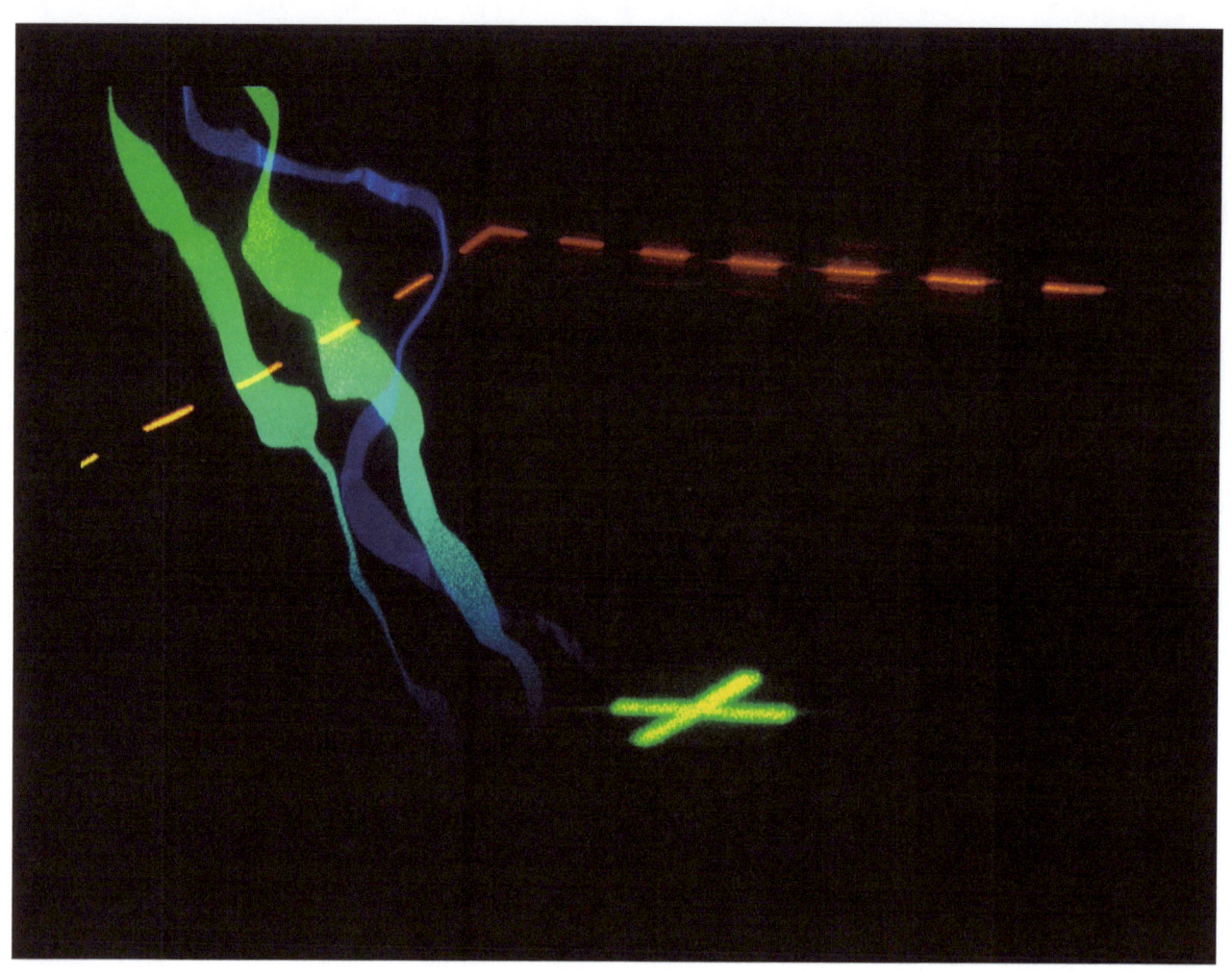

Plate 8

Delta IV, 1982

Transmission hologram: silver-halide glass plate

12 x 16 in.

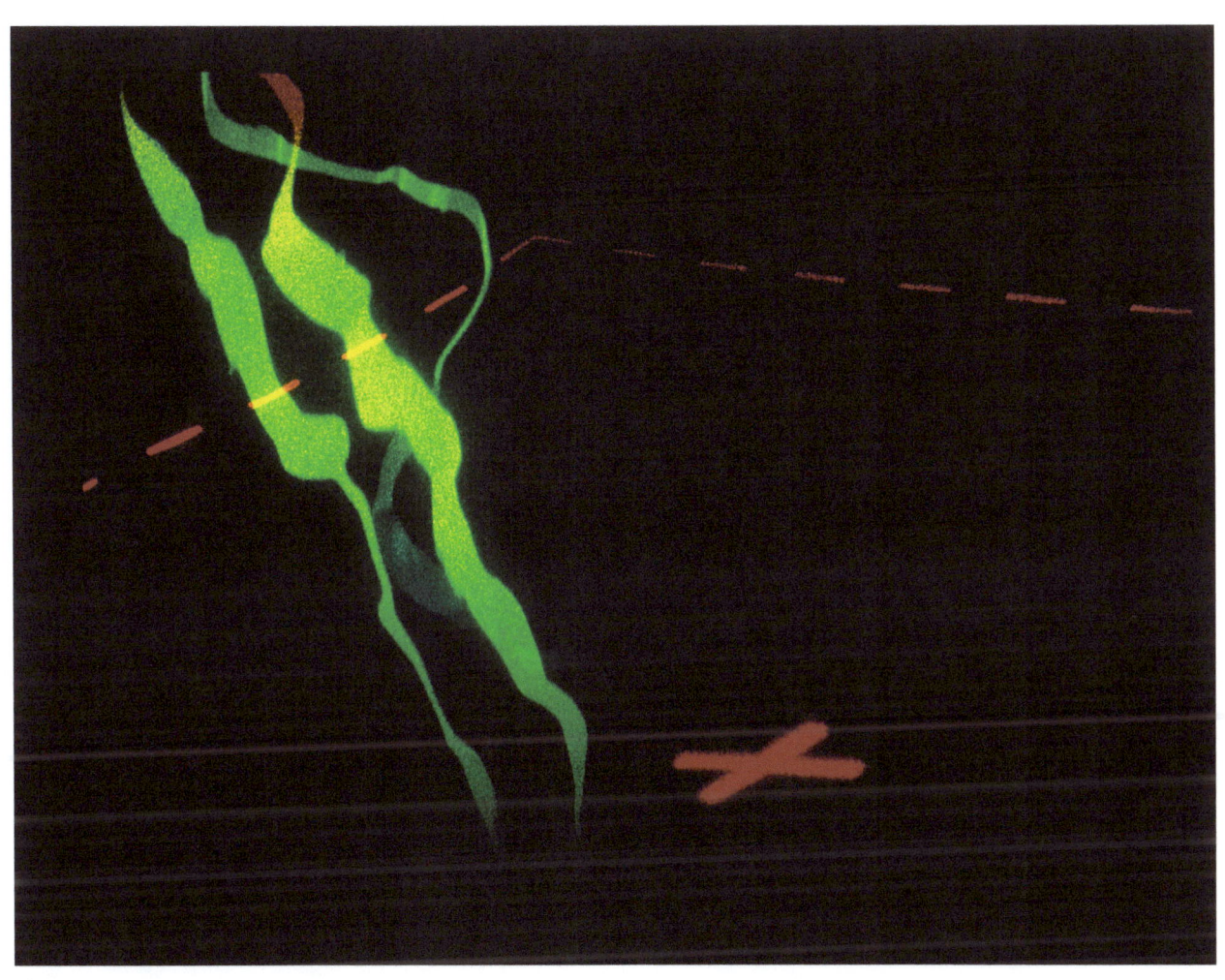

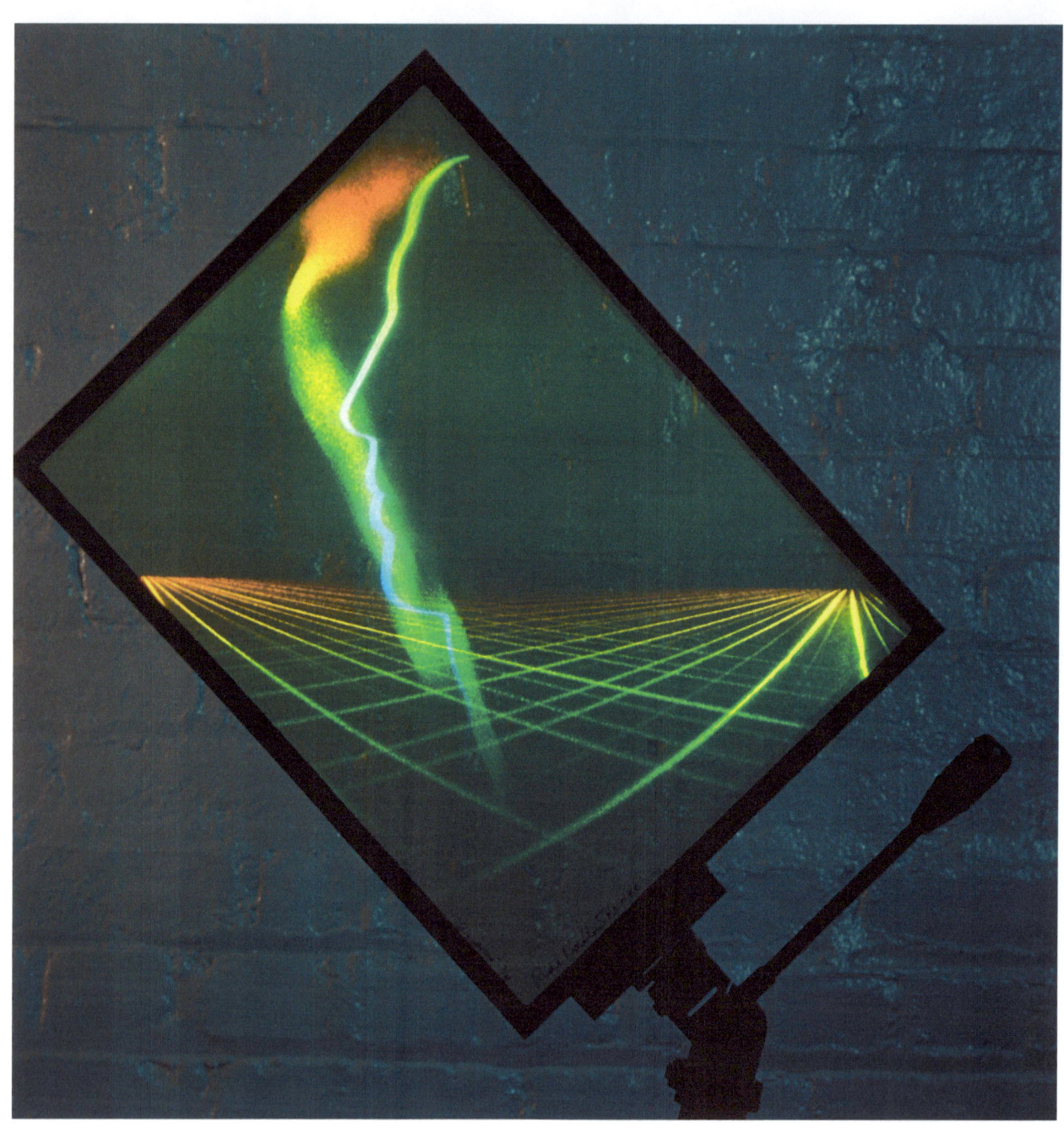

Plate 9

Wavering, 1983

Transmission hologram: silver-halide glass plate

12 x 16 in.

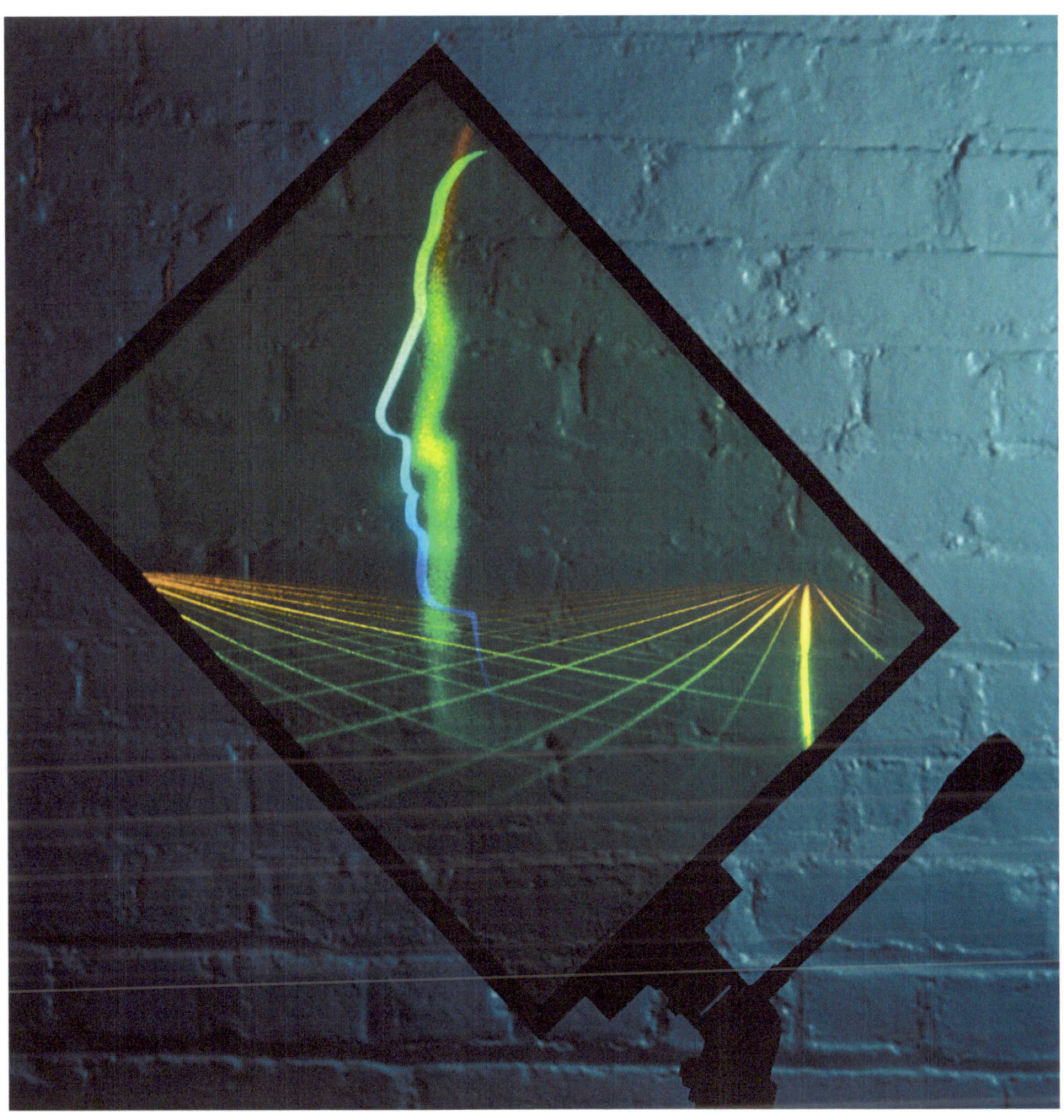

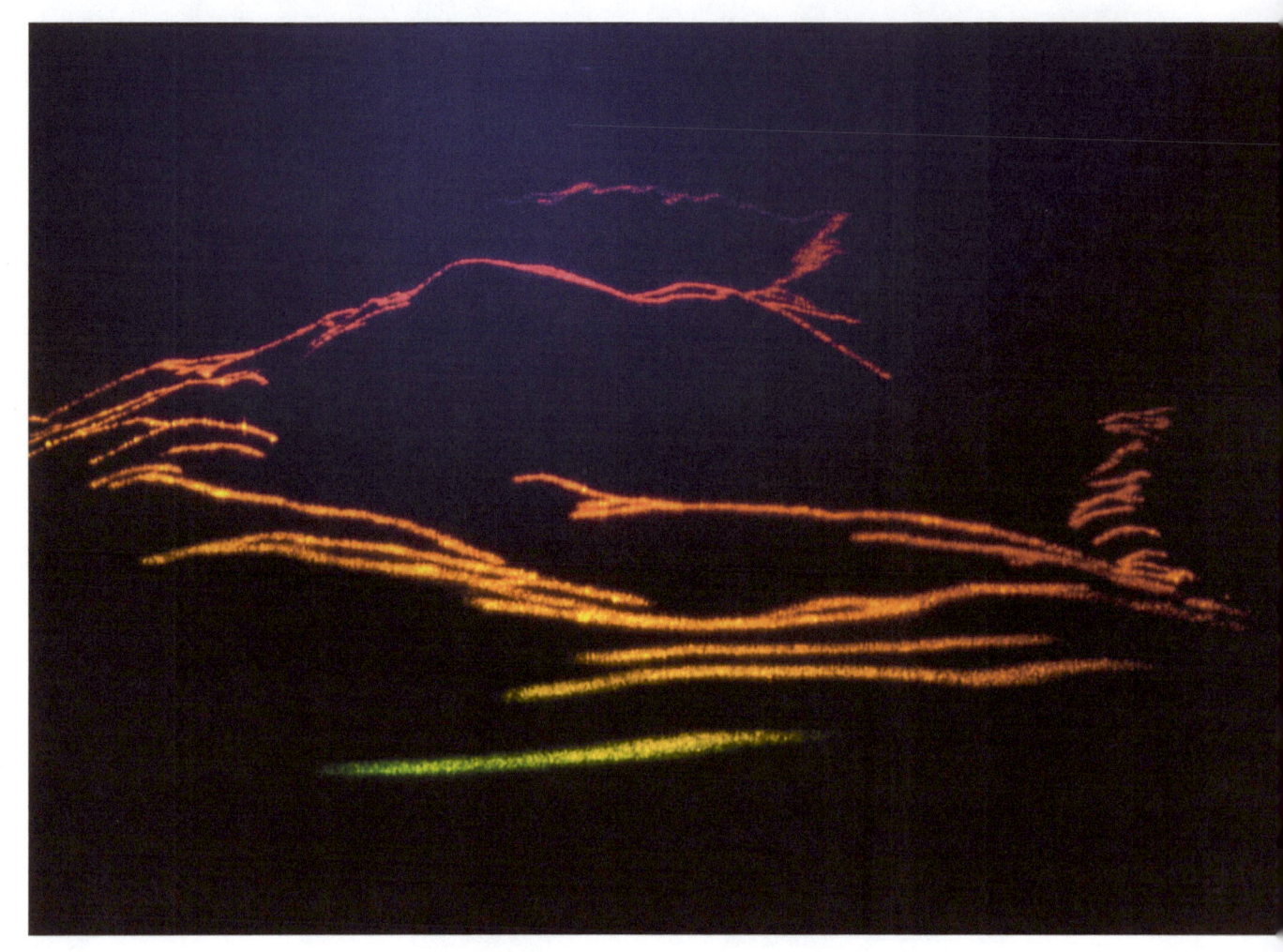

Plate 10

The New Territories, 1984

Transmission hologram: silver-halide glass plate

Two parts, each 12 x 16 in.

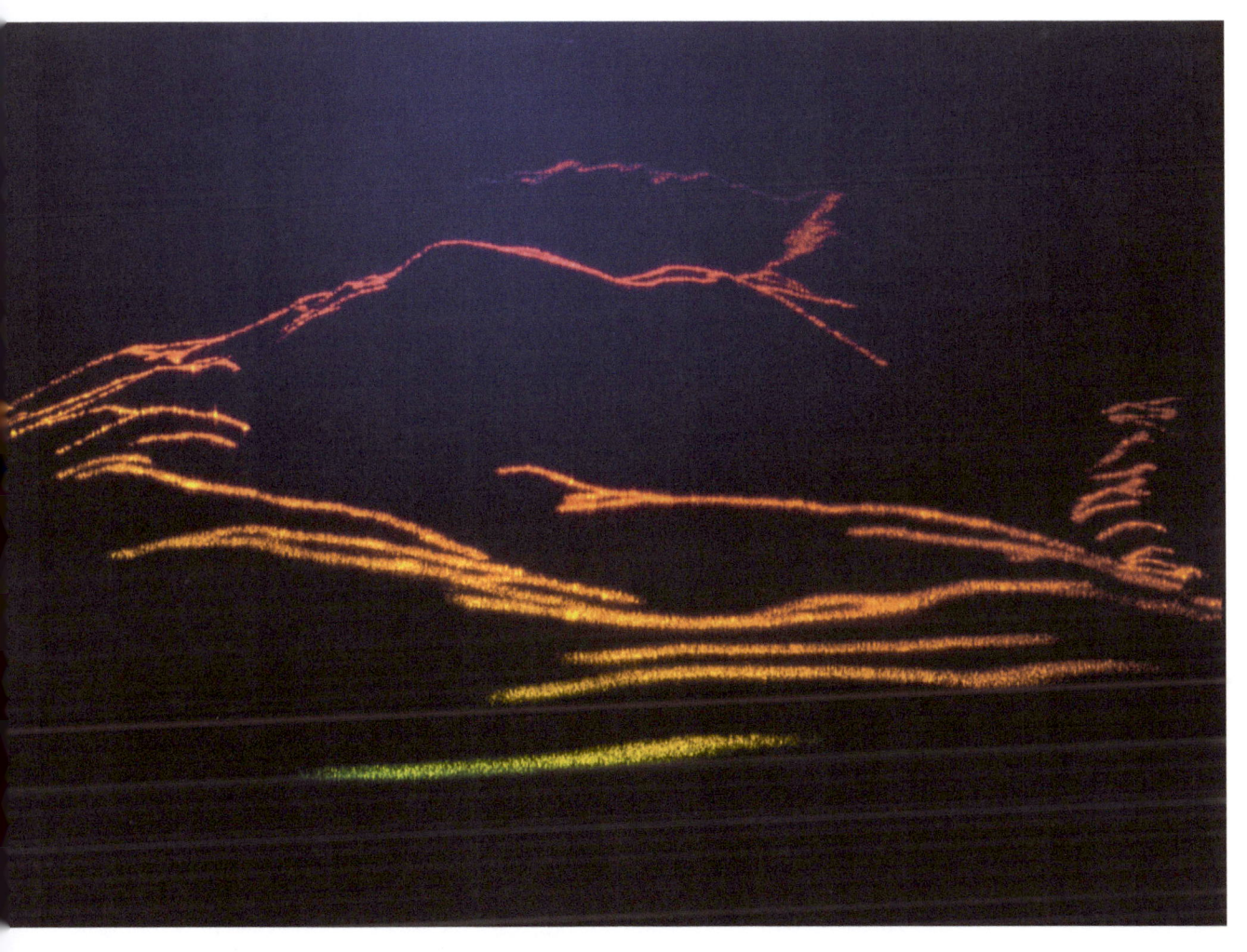

EXHIBITION CHECKLIST

RUDIE BERKHOUT
(B. NETHERLANDS, 1946–2008)

Break Even, 1989
Transmission hologram:
silver-halide glass plate
12 x 16 in.

Delta IV, 1982
Transmission hologram:
silver-halide glass plate
12 x 16 in.

Event Horizon, 1980
Transmission hologram:
silver-halide glass plate
8 x 10 in., 12 x 16 in. overall

Future Memories, 1979
Transmission hologram:
silver-halide glass plate
8 x 10 in., 12 x 16 in. overall

The New Territories, 1984
Transmission hologram:
silver-halide glass plate
Two parts, each 12 x 16 in.

Photon Study #10, 1978
Transmission hologram:
silver-halide glass plate
8 x 10 in., 12 x 16 in. overall

Toba, 1981
Transmission hologram:
silver-halide glass plate
12 x 16 in.

Transfer 137, 1980
Transmission hologram:
silver-halide glass plate
8 x 10 in., 12 x 16 in. overall

12mW Boogie, 1978
Transmission hologram:
silver-halide glass plate
Three parts, each 8 x 10 in.

Ukiyo, 1981
Transmission hologram:
silver-halide glass plate
12 x 16 in.

Wavering, 1983
Transmission hologram:
silver-halide glass plate
12 x 16 in.

All works courtesy of the Rudie Berkhout Estate

BIOGRAPHY

Solo & Two-Person Exhibitions

2014 *Holographic Collaborations: Ana Maria Nicholson and Rudie Berkhout*, Gallery 286, London

2011 *Light Years: The Art of Rudie Berkhout*, The IMC Lab + Gallery, New York

2009 *Light Magic: Rudie Berkhout*, Center for the Holographic Arts, Long Island City, NY

Legacy in Light: The Art of Rudie Berkhout, Union Mills Gallery, Catskill, NY

Rudie Berkhout, Play of Light Gallery, Catskill, NY

2001 *Odyssey 2001*, Bank of America Technology Center, Charlotte, NC

1999 *Rudie Berkhout: Holography*, Anchorage Museum of History and Art, Anchorage, AK

1993 *Holograms by Rudie Berkhout*, The Halsey Gallery at the College of Charleston, Charleston, SC

1991 *New Directions in Holography*, Whitney Museum of American Art, New York

1990 Parthenon Tama, Tama City, Japan

Art Awareness, Lexington, NY

1988 Fukuoka Art Museum, Fukuoka, Japan

1986 *The Holograms of Rudie Berkhout*, Haggerty Museum of Art, Marquette University, Milwaukee, WI

1985 *Future Memories: Holographic Work by Rudie Berkhout*, Davenport Art Gallery, Davenport, IA

Future Memories: Holographic Work by Rudie Berkhout, Lakeview Museum for Art and Science, Peoria, IL

1984 *Future Memories: Holographic Work by Rudie Berkhout*, Port Washington Library, Port Washington, NY

1983 *Future Memories: Rudie Berkhout*, James Prendergast Library, Jamestown, NY

Future Memories: Holographic Work by Rudie Berkhout, Science Museum of Virginia, Richmond, VA

Laserart La Fotografia Tridimensionale: Gli Ologrammi di Rudie Berkhout [*Laserart Three-Dimensional Photography: The Holograms of Rudie Berkhout*], Palazzo Re Enzo, Bologna, Italy

1982 Museum für Holographie und Neue Visuelle Medien, Pulheim, Germany

Palazzo Fortuny, Venice, Italy

1980 J. Fields Gallery, New York

1979 *Future Memories: Rudie Berkhout*, Museum of Holography, New York

Selected Group Exhibitions

2015 *Holocenter Summer Museum*, Center for the Holographic Arts, Governors Island, NY

2013 *Interference:Coexistence*, Center for the Holographic Arts, Long Island City, NY

Light as Medium, Ann Street Gallery, Newburgh, NY

Holography from the ZKM Collection, ZKM Center for Art and Media, Karlsruhe, Germany

2010 *Luminous Windows 2010*, MIT Museum, Cambridge, MA

2005 *Intersections: Art/Science/Mathematics*, Roland Gibson Art Gallery, Potsdam, NY

2003 SPIE Electronic Imaging Conference, Santa Clara, CA

Light from Shadow, Ivan Dougherty Gallery, Sydney, Australia

New Acquisitions 2, Gallery 286, London

2002 *Holography, The Light Fantastic*, MIT Museum, Cambridge, MA

2001 *Die verfuhrte Auge—Wege in die 3.Dimension*, Focke-Museum, Bremen, Germany

1999 *Unfolding Light: The Evolution of Ten Holographers*, Paine Art Center & Arboretum, Oshkosh, WI

Unfolding Light: The Evolution of Ten Holographers, Hofstra Museum, Hempstead, NY

1998 *Let it Flow*, The Millennium, Braunschweig, Germany

Unfolding Light: The Evolution of Ten Holographers, Salvador Dalí Museum, Saint Petersburg, FL

1997 *Unfolding Light: The Evolution of Ten Holographers*, MIT Museum, Cambridge, MA

1996 *Holographic Network*, Akademie Der Kunste, Berlin, Germany

The Nature of Light, Joyce Goldstein Gallery, New York

Bar 96, Tartessos, Barcelona, Spain

Light, Procter Art Center, Bard College, Annandale-on-Hudson, NY

1995 *Art for the End of the Century*, Humphrey Gallery, New York

New Directions in Holography, Museum of Art, Fort Worth, TX

1994 *Holography: Artists and Inventors*, MIT Museum, Cambridge, MA

One to One, Islip Museum, Dowling College, Oakdale, NY

1993 *Images du Futur*, Cite des Arts et des Nouvelles Technologies, Montreal, Canada

Regarding Beauty, School of the Arts, Charleston, SC

1992 *Olografia, Avanguardia dell'Arte Olografia*, Perugia, Italy

Hologramas, Caja del Monte, Madrid, Spain

The Edge of Light, Museum of Holography, New York

Floating Worlds, Museum of Fine Arts, Montgomery, AL

Earth and Frequencies of Life, ASTI, Washington, DC

1991 *Fourth International Exhibition of Display Holography*, Durand Art Institute, Lake Forest College, Chicago

The Holographic Center, Chicago

Raume Aus Licht, Akademie Galerie, Berlin

1990 *In Anderem Licht*, Karl Ernst Osthaus-Museum, Hagen, Germany

Wonderlight, Art, Science and Technology Institute, Washington, DC

1989 *Visiona*, High Tech in Kunst, Zurich

Artec '89, International Biennale, Nagoya, Japan

Vision and 3-D Representation, Union Gallery, Minneapolis, MN

In Glass, Forum Gallery, Minneapolis, MN

1988 *New York Holography*, Interference Gallery, Toronto

Third International Exhibition of Display Holography, Durand Art Institute, Lake Forest College, Chicago

1987 *Light Dreams: The Art and Technology of Holography*, Kalamazoo Institute of Arts, Kalamazoo, MI

1986 *Die Werklichkeit Der Bilder*, Kunsthalle, Nuremburg, Germany

FutureSight: Innovations in Art Holography, The Museum of Holography, New York

1985 *The Holographic Image: Eight Artists In The Age Of The Laser*, Gulbenkian Museum, Lisbon, Portugal

Eddies, Visual Arts Museum, School of Visual Art, New York

Mehr Licht, Kunsthalle, Hamburg, Germany

International High Technology Art Festival, Tokyo

Sculptors of Light: New York Holographic Artists, Wunsch Arts Center, New York

1984 *Invitational Exhibit*, Grace Borgenicht Gallery, New York

Holography, Technisch Museum, Amsterdam

1983 Museum of Modern Art, Hanover, Germany

Light Dimensions: The Exhibition of the Evolution of Holography, The Royal Photographic Society, Bath, England

Children's Museum, New Bedford, MA

Heller Gallery, New York

Unicorn Gallery, Aspen, CO

Lensless Photography, The Franklin Institute, Philadelphia, PA

Americans in Glass, Leigh Yawkey Woodson Art Museum, Wausau, WI

1982 Slusser Gallery, University of Michigan, Ann Arbor, MI

Dutch Artists in New York, Kling Gallery, Philadelphia

Gallery Nature Morte, New York

Light, Islip Art Museum, Islip, NY

Palazzo Re Enzo, Bologna, Italy

Contemporary Art Holography, Museum of Holography, New York

1981 Castle Gallery, College of New Rochelle, New Rochelle, NY

The Living and Learning Gallery, University of Vermont, Burlington, VT

Art of Reaction, The Katonah Gallery, Katonah, NY

Holographic Environment, McKenna Theater, State University of San Francisco, CA

1980 *Light Years Ahead: International Holography*, The Photographer's Gallery, London

FutureSight: An Exhibition of Holograms, Mediaport Gallery, Port Washington Public Library, Port Washington, NY

Beyond Object, Aspen Center for the Visual Arts, Aspen, CO

Contemporary Arts Center, New Orleans, LA

Holography 80, Chelsea School of Art, London

1979 *The Craft of Art*, Critic's Choice, Walker Art Gallery, Liverpool, England

New Spaces: The Holographer's Vision, The Franklin Institute, Philadelphia, PA

Museum of Science and History, Fort Worth, TX

Net Echt, Piazza Winkelcentrum, Eindhoven, The Netherlands

Deceiving the Eye, traveling show sponsored by Asahi Shimbun, Japan (20 venues)

Cartier Window Exhibit, Cartier, New York

1978 *Avant Garde Festival*, Cambridge, MA

As We See It, Museum of Holography, New York

Alice In the Light World, Tokyo

Reflections of Future Space, Museum of Holography, New York

The Hologram Place, 138 Gloucester Avenue, London

1977 *Avant Garde Festival*, World Trade Center, New York

Picture This, The Museum of Modern Art, New York

1976 *Through the Looking Glass*, Museum of Holography, New York

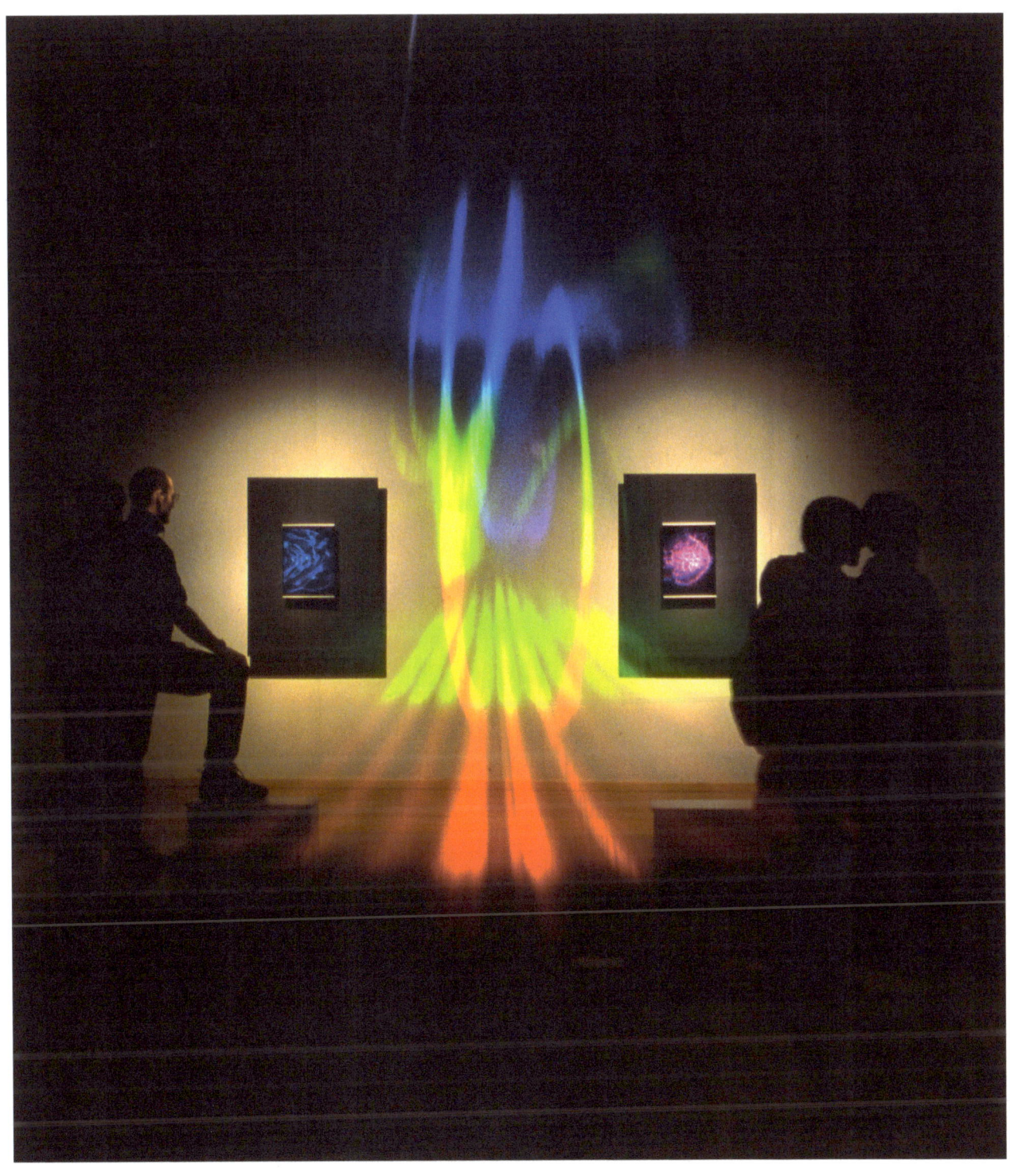

Installation view of *Rudie Berkhout: Holography*, Anchorage Museum of History and Art, 1999, photo: Chris Arend.
Courtesy Rudie Berkhout Estate.

SELECTED BIBLIOGRAPHY

Books & Catalogues

Johnston, Sean. *Holographic Visions: A History of New Science*. Oxford: Oxford University Press, 2006.

Lipp, Achim and Zec, Peter, eds. *Mehr Licht: Künstlerhologramme und Lichtobjekte [More Light: Artists's Holograms and Light Objects]*. Hamburg: Fielmann im E. Kabel Verlag, 1985.

Lucie-Smith, Edward. *Art in the Seventies*. Ithaca, NY: Cornell University Press, 1980.

Popper, Frank. *Art of the Electronic Age*. New York: Harry N. Abrams, 1993.

Ritscher, Eve. *Light Dimensions: The Exhibition of the Evolution of Holography*. London: Ardentbrook, 1983.

Walton, Paul. *Space Light: A Holography and Laser Spectacular*. London: Routledge & Kegan Paul, 1982.

Zec, Peter. *Holographie, Geschichte, Technik, Kunst*. Cologne: DuMont Buchverlag, 1987.

Zec, Peter, et al. *In Anderem Licht: Holographie Und Umraum [In a Different Light: Holography and Surroundings]*, exhibition catalogue, Munich: A11 Artforum, 1989.

Exhibition Brochures

Anchorage Museum. *Rudie Berkhout: Holography*. Anchorage, AK, 1999.

Bank of America Technology Center. *Odyssey 2001: A Collaboration: Ward Bos, Painting; Rudie Berkhout, Holography*. Charlotte, NC, 2001.

Davenport Art Gallery. *Future Memories: Rudie Berkhout*. Davenport, IA, 1985.

Franklin Institute. *New Spaces: The Holographer's Vision*. Philadelphia, PA, 1979.

James Prendergast Library. *Future Memories: Rudie Berkhout*. Jamestown, NY, 1983.

Kalamazoo Institute of Arts. *Light Dreams: The Art and Technology of Holography*. Kalamazoo, MI, 1987.

MIT Museum. *Unfolding Light: the Evolution of Ten Holographers*. Cambridge, MA, 1997.

Palazzo Re Enzo. *Laserart La Fotografia Tridimensionale: Gli Ologrammi di Rudie Berkhout* [*Laserart Three-Dimensional Photography: The Holograms of Rudie Berkhout*]. Comune di Bologna, Italy, 1983.

Patrick & Beatrice Haggerty Museum of Art. *The Holograms of Rudie Berkhout*. Marquette University, Milwaukee, WI, 1986.

Science Museum of Virginia. *Future Memories: Holographic Work by Rudy Berkhout*. Richmond, VA, 1983.

Articles & Reviews

Barilleaux, René Paul. "Holography and the Art World." *Leonardo* 25, no. 5, Archives of Holography: A Partial View of a Three-Dimensional World: Special Issue (1992): 417–418.

Benyon, Margaret. "Holography as an Art Medium." *Leonardo* 6, no. 1 (Winter 1973): 1–9.

_____. "On the Second Decade of Holography as Art and My Recent Holograms." *Leonardo* 15, no. 2 (Spring 1982): 89–95.

Berkhout, Rudie. "Holography: Exploring a New Art Realm; Shaping Empty Light with Space." *Leonardo* 22, no. 3/4, Holography as an Art Medium: Special Double Issue (1989): 313–316.

Boraiko, Allen A. "A Splendid Light: Lasers." *National Geographic* 165, no. 3 (March 1984): 335–363.

Caulfield, H. John. "The Wonder of Holography." *National Geographic* 165, no. 3 (March 1984): 365–377.

Glueck, Grace. "Art." *The New York Times*, June 1, 1984.

Goldberg, Bruce. "Holographic Art: A Critical Evaluation." *Leonardo* 22, no. 3/4, Holography as an Art Medium: Special Double Issue (1989): 417–418.

Hagen, Charles. "The Case for Holograms: The Defense Resumes." *The New York Times*, November 29, 1991.

Harrison, Helen A. "One to One: Linda Law/Rudie Berkhout." *The New York Times*, April 3, 1994.

_____. "Four Forms of Light Explored in a Delightful Show." *The New York Times*, June 13, 1982.

Klein, Jerry. "Holographic Art is Dream-Like Magic." *Journal-Star* (Peoria, IL), March 24, 1985.

Kogan, Rick. "'Wow, Cool' Describe Art's Future." *Chicago Tribune*, January 11, 1987.

Misselbeck, Reinhold. "The Museum für Holographie und neue visuelle Medien and Its Influence on Holography in Germany." *Leonardo*, 25 no. 5, Archives of Holography: A Partial View of a Three-Dimensional World: Special Issue (1992): 457–458.

"New Wave of Holographers Work to Expand the Art." *The New York Times*, July 22, 1984.

Pepper, Andrew. "Rudie Berkhout: Artist/Scientist." *Holosphere* 9, no. 11 (November 1980): 3–4.

Raynor, Vivian. "Art; Technology as a Medium for Artists." *The New York Times*, February 22, 1981.

Razutis, Al. "Conversation with Rudie Berkhout." *Wavefront Magazine* 1, no. 1, (Winter 1985), accessed September 8, 2015. http://www.alchemists.com/visual_alchemy/wavefront/wave29.html

Shepard, Richard F. "Holography Takes Root in SoHo in a Museum Devoted to Future." *The New York Times*, December 29, 1976.

Sozanski, Edward J. "When Art, Science And Gadgetry Cross Paths; Art For The End Of The Century Explores The Territory Of High-Tech Art." *Philadelphia Inquirer*, August 18, 1995.

Woodburn, Judith P. "The Light Fantastic." *Milwaukee Magazine* (February 1986): 103–105.

ACKNOWLEDGMENTS

The exhibition and catalogue would not have been possible without the enthusiastic participation and generous support of the following individuals

Hudson Talbott

Fred Berkhout

Henriette Berkhout

Martina Mrongovius

Hart Perry

Michael Gabor

Amanda Collier

Linda Law

Jay Lesenger

Tom Ditto

Melissa Crenshaw

Jon Seymour

Harun Adonis Triplett

Susan DeMaio Smutny

Catherine Herne

Jeffrey Peltzman

Curatorial and editorial research and assistance

Danielle Epstein

Amanda Henneberry

Maggie Quinn

Reproduction rights courtesy

The Rudie Berkhout Estate

Ashley M. Morton, Managing Account Executive, Editorial Sales Domestic, National Geographic Creative

Rachael Robinson, Curatorial Associate, Museum Reference & Hart Nautical Collections, MIT Museum

Photo credits

Chris Arend:
(pages 48–49)

Rudie Berkhout:
12mW Boogie (pages 52–53)
Future Memories (page 55)
Transfer 137 (pages 56–57)

Michael Gabor:
Photon Study #10 (pages 50–51)
Event Horizon (pages 58–59)
Ukiyo (pages 60–61)
Toba (page 62–63)

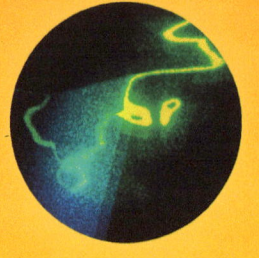